EVERYTHING KIDS' Basketball Book

The all-time greats, legendary teams, today's superstars—and tips on playing like a pro

Bob Schaller

with Coach Dave Harnish

Adams media
Avon, Massachusetts

PUBLISHER Karen Cooper

DIRECTOR OF ACQUISITIONS AND INNOVATION Paula Munier

MANAGING EDITOR, EVERYTHING® SERIES Lisa Laing

COPY CHIEF Casey Ebert

ACQUISITIONS EDITOR Katrina Schroeder

SENIOR DEVELOPMENT EDITOR Brett Palana-Shanahan

ASSOCIATE DEVELOPMENT EDITOR Elizabeth Kassab

EDITORIAL ASSISTANT Hillary Thompson

EVERYTHING® SERIES COVER DESIGNER Erin Alexander

LAYOUT DESIGNERS Colleen Cunningham, Elisabeth Lariviere, Ashley Vierra, Denise Wallace

An Everything® Series Book.
Everything® and everything.com® are registered trademarks of F+W Media, Inc.

Published by Adams Media, a division of F+W Media, Inc.
57 Littlefield Street, Avon, MA 02322. U.S.A.
www.adamsmedia.com

ISBN-10: 1-60550-165-4
ISBN-13: 978-1-60550-165-9

Printed by RR Donnelley, Harrisonburg, VA, USA

10   9   8   7   6

June 2014

This publication is designed to provide accurate and authoritative information with regard to the subject matter covered. It is sold with the understanding that the publisher is not engaged in rendering legal, accounting, or other professional advice. If legal advice or other expert assistance is required, the services of a competent professional person should be sought.
—From a *Declaration of Principles* jointly adopted by a Committee of the American Bar Association and a Committee of Publishers and Associations

Many of the designations used by manufacturers and sellers to distinguish their products are claimed as trademarks. When those designations appear in this book and Adams Media was aware of a trademark claim, the designations have been printed with initial capital letters.

Interior illustrations by Kurt Dolber.
Puzzles by Beth L. Blair.

This book is available at quantity discounts for bulk purchases.
For information, please call 1-800-289-0963.

Visit the entire Everything® series at *www.everything.com*

Contents

☆ 🏀 ☆

1

Playing the Game

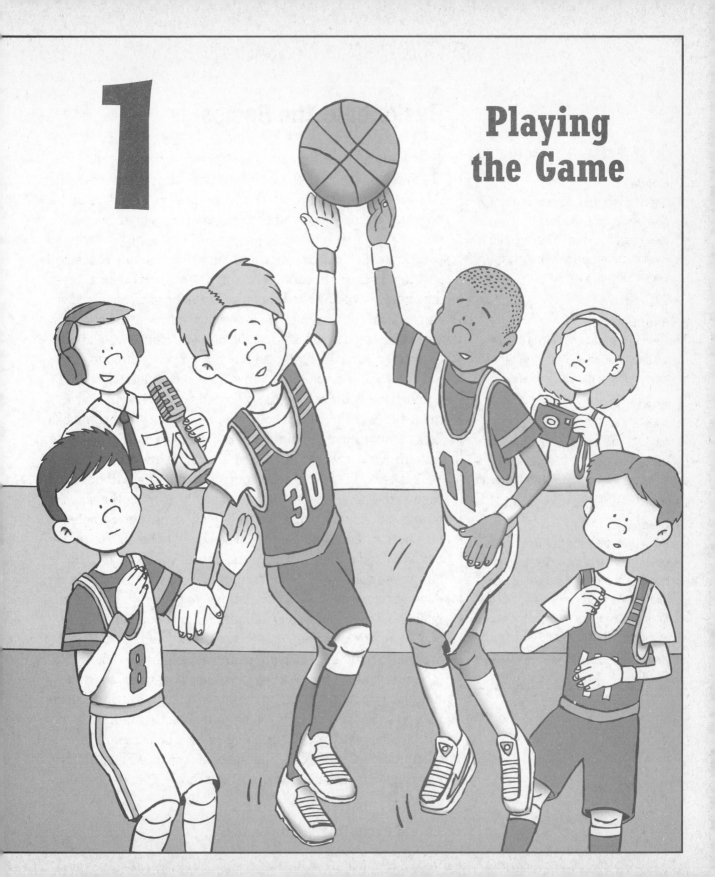

WORDS TO KNOW

Hustle

The term "hustle" means try harder, never give up. When coaches yell for their players to hustle during practices and games, they are telling their players to keep working hard and not slack off.

Rebound

Getting the ball after it hits the rim on an unsuccessful shot on either the defensive or offensive end.

Assist

A pass that sets up a successful basket. The player who made that pass is credited with an assist. Usually, the point guard will be the team leader in assists.

Steal

When you take the ball from the other team, it is recorded for statistical purposes as a steal. You can intercept a pass or actually take it from a player who is dribbling carelessly or out of control. Racking up a lot of steals shows you are a good defender.

Basketball: The Basics

Basketball can seem like a very complex game. Maybe you've seen a coach draw a squiggly diagram to show what he wants to do. If you've watched the game on TV, you've probably noticed that the commentators draw lines on the screen during a game to show what happened. How do all of these people know exactly what's going on? Simple! At its core, basketball isn't that hard. It's about hustling on defense and offense, paying attention, taking good shots, and making good passes. If you can do all of those things, you're well on your way to becoming a good basketball player. To be the best you can be, you'll need to focus on fundamentals and practice proper technique.

The goal in playing the game is even simpler: Score more points than your opponent. Some people say the goal is to make more baskets than your opponents, but since some baskets are worth three points and others are worth two—and free throws are worth only one—that's not always the case.

Basketball is played on a court with a basketball hoop at each end. There are five players for each team on the court at a time. Unlike sports like football, players need to be able to play both offense and defense. They need to be able to make baskets to give their team points, but they also need to be able to stop the other team from making baskets at the other end of the court. To be a good offensive player, you'll need to know how to dribble, pass, rebound, and shoot. On defense, you'll need to know how to rebound, steal, and play all-around good defense, which means never getting lazy.

Basketball is a fun sport because even if you miss the first time you go out and shoot, by the end of an hour or two you'll be making shots fairly often if you pay attention to your form. You can also get pretty good at dribbling in a hurry. Basketball is a sport that many people play because it's easy to learn and there are usually basketball hoops in parks, schools, gyms, and even driveways.

Basketballs vary in size. College and professional players use larger balls than kids. The women's basketball is slightly smaller than the one the men play with. You can usually get a good basketball at your favorite local discount store. If you are using it outside, make sure you get one made out of a synthetic or rubber-like cover rather than the leather ball used for indoor courts; these balls are more durable than the ones you use indoors. Once you have some athletic shoes and a ball, you are ready to get started.

Players by Position

There are five players on the court at any given time for each team. Here are the players and their roles, and this is for any level, from amateur through college and professional.

Point Guard

Called the "one" spot, the point guard is usually the smallest and/or quickest player on the team. He also acts as the coach on the floor and the quarterback of the team, getting his teammates organized and deciding what to do with the ball. He must be an excellent ball handler and passer who plays with bounce and enthusiasm. Good point guards are usually tough and strong players who love to practice. More often than not, they are confident, competitive, poised, and fearless.

Point guards can be counted on to understand the coach's system and know that games are won on the inside, around the basket. They also realize that scoring is not their top priority. The point guard plays in front of his teammates on both ends of the floor. He is the take-charge person who encourages teammates and gets them to respond. He has

FUN FACTS

Basketball was embraced as a U.S. high school sport in the early 1900s for one reason: It didn't cost much to provide equipment and space to play. Student athletes needed only tennis shoes, T-shirts, and shorts, and schools installed backboards, hoops, and painted lines on playgrounds and in high school gymnasiums.

TIP-IN

Basketball shoes have become big business since the introduction of the Air Jordan, a shoe Michael Jordan introduced for Nike. You only need shoes that are comfortable and don't hurt your feet. It's cool to wear what the pros wear, but you'll play your best in shoes that feel good rather than ones that look good or have your favorite player's name on them.

Name That Position

There's a lot of skill involved in being a good basketball player. First, you have to know your position. Someone has forgotten the full names here. Can you fill in the blanks?

_____ guard
(usually best ball thrower from a distance)

_____ forward
(tend to be versatile)

_____ forward
(usually not as tall as the center)

_____ guard
(usually shortest and fastest)

_____
(usually tallest and slowest)

ELEPHANT BALL

What's the difference between an elephant and a basketball?

One is big and round and charges through nets and the other is a basketball!

great court vision and freely gives up the ball to the first open teammate. A point guard must be able to lead the team in assists each season and be able to come through in the clutch by handling the ball in the final moments of a close game. He must be able to make high-pressure free throws if he is fouled in the closing minutes of a tough game. Point guards are rarely the leading scorers on the team since they have other responsibilities, but they should average 10–12 points and at least five assists per game.

Shooting Guard

The shooting guard, or "two," must be a very versatile player. She is usually the biggest of the two guards and the best shooter on the team. She is a scorer who can both take the ball to the basket and make the outside shot with regularity. Shooting guards are expected to be excellent outside shooters to 20 feet. Also known as an off guard, she should be a very good ball handler, capable of rushing the ball up the court on a fast break or ready to take over for the point guard in breaking the opponent's defense and running the offense. The off guard should be the second best passer on the team and should be capable of playing great defense to stop the other team's shooting guard. A shooting guard must understand what shots the coach wants her to take. She must be willing to take and make a good percentage of the big shots late in the game.

Small Forward

The "three," as it is known, is probably the most athletic position on the team because the small forward must be able to play inside the key area by the basket and shoot from the outside, too. Usually the smaller of the two forwards, the small forward must be capable of rebounding and scoring against taller players. He must be able to handle the ball outside on the perimeter against smaller players. This position is

TIP-IN

Before he became an NBA coach, Scott Skiles was one of the best passing guards in the league. He played for the Orlando Magic in 1990 and set a record for most assists in a game. He had 30 against the Denver Nuggets on December 30, 1990.

FUN FACTS

Derrick Rose led Memphis to the NCAA championship game in 2008. The Chicago Bulls selected him as the first overall pick in the draft that year, and he snagged the NBA's Rookie of the Year award in 2009. In his first playoff game, he scored 36 points against the Boston Celtics—a record for a rookie in his first playoff game.

WORDS TO KNOW

Playmaker
This is a term used to describe a player who either sets up plays with smart passes that lead to baskets or takes the ball and scores after receiving it. The playmaker has the ability to put points on the board in situations where scoring a basket seems unlikely.

★ **FUN FACTS** ★

LeBron James is one of the most widely regarded small forwards in the NBA today. He was drafted by the Cleveland Cavaliers as the number one overall pick in the 2003 draft and was named the NBA's Most Valuable Player in the 2008–2009 season. LeBron is a versatile player who is one of the league's top scorers and free throw shooters.

one of the more physically demanding, and the player needs to be both tough and aggressive in rebounding to compensate for lack of size. The ideal small forward should average five to seven rebounds per game and have an excellent jump shot, along with the ability to drive and score in traffic. The small forward requires a player who can run and fill the lane on a fast break—a fast break is when the team gets the ball near their basket and runs toward the other end of the court with the ball, also known as breaking fast up the court. A small forward must also help against presses, which is when a defensive team comes into their opponents' end of the floor to guard them all the way up the court into the offensive end rather than just running back and waiting for the team with the ball to come into their end of the court. The small forward must also be disciplined enough to rebound missed shots. Because of the versatility required to play this position, the small forward often becomes the leading scorer on the team.

Power Forward

This is called the "four" position, usually the tallest or strongest of the two forwards. The power forward is usually a player who likes physical play and has a shooting range of 15 feet. They can be intimidating players and have to play with an attitude that they will out-work and out-hustle their opponents. A true power forward knows that the success of the team depends on his ability to become a dominant force and top rebounder. They should average seven to nine rebounds per game at the college or professional level; they should be one of the two leading rebounders on the team, along with the center. They are the best offensive rebounders on the team, scoring the majority of their points off the offensive board and in the lane, the area in the free throw box on either side of the basket. You will see players run through the lane with the ball to score or jump through the lane to get rebounds.

Power forwards are the best outlet passers; an outlet pass is thrown by the player who gets the rebound after a missed shot. This outlet pass can result in a "fast break" where the players rush the ball up the court so that the defense on the other team does not have the time to set up properly. Depending on the fast break, they cover defensively on an inside post player. The post is the area on either side of the free throw line. It's where players who dunk usually get the ball because they are only five to eight feet from the hoop when someone passes them the ball. Power forwards are able to anticipate when a shot will be taken so they can start to the board early to rebound.

Center

This is called the "five" spot. Many people believe that this is the most difficult position to play because of short reaction time caused by congestion in the lane and the fact that the player must perform offensively with her back to the basket. The center is normally the tallest player on the team and the most effective player with her back to the basket. Strength is a very important part of playing this position. The center needs to be able to muscle her way to a position where she can receive the ball and score even with several players around her.

Good teams try to pass the ball inside on about every fourth pass, so centers should also lead in the number of free-throw attempts. The center must be able to use her body to establish position so her teammates can collapse the defense by getting the ball inside. Shooting range is not particularly important to playing this position, but it's critical for the center to learn the basic post moves and be able to decide when to use each move. The center should rival the power forward for the most number of rebounds. The center is the last line of defense before the basket, and must be willing to help teammates defensively

FUN FACTS

The Atlanta Dream selected Louisville forward Angel McCoughtry as the first overall pick in the 2009 WNBA draft. Angel helped lead the Cardinals to the NCAA championship game in 2009. In college, Angel was an All-American in 2008 and averaged 20 points, 9.1 rebounds, and 3.5 steals in four years at Louisville.

WORDS TO KNOW

Blocks
A blocked shot is a ball that is swatted away or knocked down as the player is taking a shot. If the ball is already on its way down toward the hoop when it is blocked, it is called goaltending, and the basket counts even if it does not go in.

by blocking shots or taking a charge on opposing players when they attempt to drive to the basket. A charge is when a defensive player has both feet planted and an offensive player with the ball runs into her. If the defender's feet are not planted firmly in place, she will be called for a "block" or blocking the person with the ball. However, a fast defender can anticipate where the player with the ball is going, get to that place first, and draw the foul on the offensive player.

Offense

If you are going to have an offense, you have to be able to score. To score, you have to be able to make shots. And to get good shots, you need to know how to dribble, pass, and shoot the basketball. Once you know these principles and practice them, you will be able to develop your offensive skills.

Shooting is something you have to practice a lot to get good at. Face the basket when you shoot the ball. Place your feet about a shoulder width apart, bend your knees slightly, and keep your back straight. Hold the ball in your shooting hand, but position the other hand on the side of the ball to help guide the shot. You shoot the ball more with your fingertips, so you don't want the ball in the palm of your hand when you shoot it. Think about keeping the ball from resting in the palm of your hand and always using your fingertips.

To be a good offensive player, you'll need to master the following types of shots:

- **Jump shot.** Taken from the standing position, you jump as you shoot the ball. Jumping gives you more power and range and helps prevent opposing players from blocking your shot. By jumping, you can shoot over your opponent. The jump shot is the most common type of shot.

- **Set shot.** Taken from the standing position, your feet do not leave the floor. A free throw is considered a set shot.
- **Layup.** This occurs when a player is dribbling very close to the basket, approaching it from the left or right side rather than straight on. You will often use the backboard to bank the ball into the basket.

Passing

Passing is one of the most important parts of the game. You can pass the ball to open players to get better shots or to players who are not being guarded by opponents. You often step forward as you pass to generate power; however, you can also pass while you are standing still if someone is open and you don't need a lot of force to get the ball to him quickly.

When you watch a game, see if you can identify the following types of passes:

- **Chest pass.** The ball is passed from the passer's chest to the receiver's chest.
- **Bounce pass.** The passer throws the ball and it bounces about two-thirds of the way toward the receiver. Typically, the bounce pass takes longer to complete, though it is harder to intercept because defenders usually hold their hands up to block chest passes and shots. The bounce pass is used to throw the ball around defenders.
- **Overhead pass.** Use this type of pass to throw the ball over your defenders; you will use two hands to pass the ball from over your head.
- **Outlet pass.** This type of pass can be thrown to move the ball rapidly up the floor and may be thrown using one arm, baseball style.
- **No-look pass.** This is for advanced players, and is used to keep the opposing player from knowing where you will pass the ball. This is a high-risk pass and should only be

WORDS TO KNOW

Brick
A shot that misses the rim and bounces hard off the backboard. The shot is different from an air ball because an air ball misses everything, whereas the brick hits something—and hits it hard. Players without a good arc to their shots are more likely to shoot bricks. Players who shoot a lot of bricks are called "bricklayers."

Air ball
The term used when the ball is shot, misses the rim, and touches neither the rim nor the backboard. Even though the player missed the basket by a long shot, it is not considered good sportsmanship for crowds to chant "Air ball," especially at a children's game.

Bank shot
Think of bouncing a paper ball off the wall into a trashcan. A bank shot gives you a chance to aim at something you can see on the backboard. A bank shot is also harder to block because the player defending you usually anticipates the shot going toward the rim, not toward a spot on the backboard.

WORDS TO KNOW

Behind-the-back pass
In a behind-the-back pass, you pass the ball from your right hand to your left by pushing the ball behind your back. These are hard to do accurately and are often intercepted, and even your teammates might not be expecting the ball. Learn to do the basic passes well first.

used with coach's approval and once you have thoroughly mastered it and all other passes.

You can also pass off the dribble. Instead of dribbling the ball to yourself, you can push it to one of your teammates. It is similar to a bounce pass, but you won't interrupt your dribble to hold the ball before passing it. It's a hard pass to master, but it catches defenses off guard because they do not have time to prepare to defend it or intercept the ball.

Dribbling

Quite simply, dribbling means bouncing the ball. It's an important skill to master because you must dribble the ball if you want to walk or run while you have it. To dribble, you push the ball toward the court rather than patting it. This gives you more control while you dribble. The best dribblers can run up and down the court bouncing the ball the whole way.

A good dribbler bounces the ball low to the ground, which makes it more difficult for the defender to steal it. To be a good dribbler, you need to be able to use either hand to dribble. Practice changing hands and changing directions to make it harder for defenders to predict where the ball is going. Some players can dribble behind their backs or between their legs. One key dribbling move is called the crossover. A crossover sounds simple enough: you move the ball from one hand to the other while dribbling. But your defender isn't prepared for the change in direction, which makes it harder for her to stop you or steal the ball.

Practice dribbling until you can do it without looking at the ball. Learn to use your peripheral vision to see the floor. This allows you to focus on looking for open teammates to pass to or a good shot at the basket.

★ FUN FACTS ★

Ever notice how basketball shoes look different from regular tennis shoes? The top on basketball shoes goes up higher to provide ankle support for all the running, jumping, and cutting basketball players do. These shoes are called high tops because the top goes up higher than standard tennis shoes.

Developing Offensive Skills

Sure, some kids are born bigger, stronger, and with more physical ability than others. But even the great basketball players like LeBron James, Michael Jordan, Larry Bird, and Magic Johnson had to practice to get as good as they are. They had to work hard to achieve success. Basketball players are not born; they are made in the driveway and gymnasium and on the playground.

Even though plays can be diagrammed in hundreds of different ways, basketball's simplicity is part of its beauty. A kid who wants to become a better dribbler needs only a basketball and a hard, flat surface. If you want to work on shots from all over, all you need is a ball and a hoop. Conditioning for the sport involves a lot of running, which can be done almost anywhere—outside of the house, please!

To ensure you are on the right track to becoming a successful basketball player, try these:

- Shoot a layup from either side of the basket.
- Dribble the length of the court using either hand. Keep your head up; don't look at the ball.
- Shoot a jump shot from 8 to 12 feet away from the basket after catching a pass.
- Dribble to within 8 to 12 feet of the basket and shoot a shot from there.
- Make a two-handed chest pass, approximately 15 feet, to a moving target.
- Make five out of 10 free throws from 12 feet away. Then practice until you can make five out of 10 free throws from the regulation 15-foot free throw line.

WORDS TO KNOW

Double dribble
Double dribbling means you start dribbling, stop, and start dribbling again. This is not allowed, and if you get called for it, you have to turn the ball over to the other team. Don't stop dribbling unless you are ready to shoot or make a pass. Once you stop dribbling, do not even think about dribbling again as an option.

Basketball Position

The proper basketball position is important to master when you first start playing. A proper base position is like the foundation of a house—it holds everything up. A bad base position will cause you problems defending, shooting, and scoring.

What to Do with Your Legs

To get into the proper basketball position, bend your knees, place feet about shoulder-width apart, and raise your hands to about chest or shoulder level. Getting in this position keeps you balanced. If you are standing straight up, you won't be able to react quickly, whether it's to catch or intercept a pass, break toward a basket, get open, or move to cover an opponent. Having your knees slightly bent allows you to spring into action.

Keeping your feet apart allows you the best balance. You are also ready to take off running. You generally want to have one foot slightly in front of the other foot. This staggered stance allows you a better reaction time.

Your feet are just as important as your arms in basketball. When you are playing defense, you never want to cross one foot over the other when guarding a player. If you do, your opponent can catch you off-stride and change direction on you. For example, if you are moving to your right and you use your left foot to step over your right foot, your opponent will cut to your left and leave you in the dust. By moving your feet in a shuffling manner and never crossing over, you can keep your opponent in front of you and make it harder for her to escape you.

What to Do with Your Arms

Keep your arms close to your chest. This allows your wrists and hands to be in the proper position to catch the ball. You also want to keep your head neither too far forward nor too far backward. Think of it as a line running down your head through the middle of your body to the floor. That's the proper basketball position. If your hands are on your hips or by your side, you will be caught off guard if a pass or a rebound comes toward you.

Basketball Speed

It's funny, but track stars aren't often great basketball players. You don't have to be a fast runner to be a basketball player. It is more important to be a good player and be quick than to be really fast. You need to move to the right place on the floor rather than just sprint up and down. Knowing where you need to be and staying in the proper basketball position will usually allow you to get to the right place more quickly than someone who is a faster runner than you are. You need to work on your starts and stops, your pivots, and changing direction. These are not difficult things to master, but they take a lot of practice.

First things first: When you change direction, you want to be low and turn your head in the direction you want to go. If you are heading left, take that first step with your left foot; if you are going right, take off with your right foot first.

You need to be able to change direction and stop immediately. The ball doesn't simply go up and down the court, back and forth. Drills that boost your agility will help your balance. If you lose your balance, you are likely to stumble, commit a foul, double dribble, or be out of position. A big part of the game is practicing how to stop quickly and change direction.

When you pivot, you have one foot planted. This is called your pivot foot. You want to be on the ball of your pivot foot to allow you to move around to find a person to pass to or position yourself for a shot. You should learn to pivot on both feet.

Defense

Solid defense isn't as dazzling as offense, and not many defensive plays make the highlight reels. However, defense is just as important to the game as offense. A good

WORDS TO KNOW

Switch
When you are playing defense, you might hear one of your teammates yell, "Switch!" This means she wants to guard the player you are guarding and you should guard her opponent.

defense can keep your opponent from making baskets, and it's very hard to win if you don't get any points. Defense is a state of mind and attitude. The amount of hustle and sound fundamentals are the most important thing, even more important than natural talent.

Defense Matters

Coaches are known to say that offense wins games, but defense wins championships. There is nothing more important in the game of basketball than being able to keep an opposing team from scoring points. Many players through the years have made their whole career on playing great defense. Some of the greatest defenders don't score a lot, but they have long careers because they are able to keep the other team from scoring.

Being a great rebounder is a way to develop into being a solid defensive player. Being able to steal passes is another way to defend well. Another way is to be able to cover a player who is trying to pass a ball and either prevent him from passing it or force him to throw the ball away.

Defensive Strategies

There are all kinds of defenses that coaches use. The two main ones are the zone defense and man-to-man defense.

In zone defense, the court is divided into zones and each player is responsible for a particular area. For example, a guard might be responsible for an area on the perimeter or out around the free throw line. If an opponent comes into that area, the guard covers him until he moves out of that particular zone. The same thing goes for near the basket, where forwards and centers will have particular zones.

Man-to-man defense is much simpler, yet much more constant work for defenders. In man-to-man defense, each player is responsible for guarding a specific player on the other team. So wherever that player goes, the defensive player goes, too.

Be a Good Defender!

If you want to play good defense in general, you need to have or develop good footwork. It's important that you know which way to face and when and where to turn. A good defender needs to become a little bit of a psychic. You have to think about what you know about basketball and use that to guess when another player might make a pass or take a shot. If you can do this, you can put pressure on your opponent and try to block the shot or pass. Good defenders are so good at pressuring their opponents that sometimes they can force another player to make a bad shot or turn over the ball. You can become a good defender by learning how to position yourself between the basket and an offensive player. That way, when your opponent misses a shot, you get the inside track toward a rebound. Practice this by having someone shoot baskets and stand near the hoop so you can see how and where the ball comes off the rim.

Basketball Position and Defense

You want to be in the basketball position at all times on defense. You must stay lower than the player you are guarding. If you are standing upright, the player will go around you. You always want your head to be lower than the head of the player you are guarding.

Keep your weight balanced so that you're not leaning too far forward at any time. If your head is lower, your opponent will not be able to charge past you because he will have to lower his head to start that move. This gives you the advantage because you can react before he even thinks of getting past you, and you can continue to remain in front of him.

You should have one foot forward. Your front foot should be on the ball handler's weakest side. If he is right handed, your left foot should be forward to force him to put the ball in his left hand.

FUN FACTS

Kevin Garnett was voted NBA Defensive Player of the Year in 2008, the same year his Boston Celtics won the championship. Kevin is known for getting rebounds and making big blocks. He has had eight blocks in a single game twice in his career and averages 8½ rebounds per game.

Same But Different

Offensive and defensive plays all have special names so the team knows what they're doing. These teams have the same number of plays but not the exact same plays. Can you find the two plays on each court that don't appear on the other team's court?

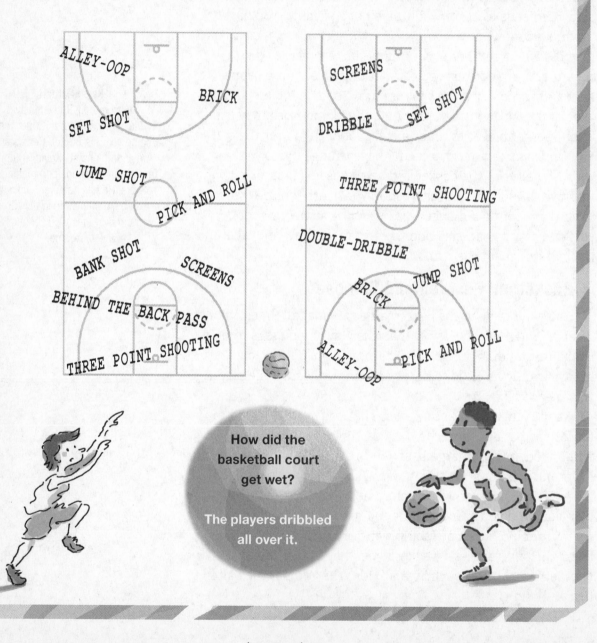

ALLEY-OOP
BRICK
SET SHOT
JUMP SHOT
PICK AND ROLL
BANK SHOT
SCREENS
BEHIND THE BACK PASS
THREE POINT SHOOTING

SCREENS
DRIBBLE
SET SHOT
THREE POINT SHOOTING
DOUBLE-DRIBBLE
BRICK
JUMP SHOT
ALLEY-OOP
PICK AND ROLL

How did the basketball court get wet?

The players dribbled all over it.

Always position yourself between the ball handler and the basket. If the ball handler gets past you, get your body back in front of him and between him and the basket. Since you don't have the basketball, you should be able to run faster than the player who is dribbling the ball.

When he stops dribbling, attack the player with good basketball stance and keep your hands moving to make it harder for the player to pass. Hopefully, you can create a turnover.

Stand By Your Man

You also want to stay close to your man, in what is commonly called the player's "bubble," an area two or three feet around the player. This will make him work to get around you. However, if you are too close and bump into him, you will be called for a foul. If you are right on top of him, it makes it easier for him to go past you on your left or right. You want to be in an area close enough to your opponent that you can knock the ball away or deflect a pass attempt, but not so close that you are in danger of bumping into him.

Keeping your hands up while you defend is important. It gives you a chance to knock away a pass or steal the ball off the dribble. Having your hands up also blocks part of your opponent's field of vision. If you are good with your feet and see a pass coming off a dribble, you can shuffle over and reach out with your hands to prevent a pass.

You want to force the ball handler to go in a direction he doesn't want to go by positioning yourself in his path and steering him off course, forcing him to make an unplanned decision or pass.

Even if you are not guarding the ball handler, your job is still important. You want to position yourself to keep the player you are guarding from getting the ball. Keep your hand and arm in the passing lane so you can knock away a pass or force the ball handler to choose someone else to try to pass the ball to.

TIP-IN

When you are guarding a player taller than you, it's more important than ever to be in the right position. You might be faster than the taller player, so when he moves you might be able to stay one step ahead of him and prevent him from receiving a pass.

Fouls

A foul is called when illegal contact is made or a rule is violated. You can be called for a foul if you are on offense or defense, so you always need to be aware of what you can and cannot do. If you are trying to steal the ball and you smack the ball handler's hand, you will be called for a foul. If you run into a defender who is standing in one place and has position (which means he has both feet planted and not moving), you will get whistled for a foul. If you reach over a player's back, push a player, hit a player on the head when you try to block a shot, or jump toward a player and land on him while he is shooting, you will get called for a foul.

That is why being a basketball player with proper position and fundamentals is so important. By following the guidelines, you won't put yourself in a position to commit a foul. Fouls can hurt a team in a few different ways. A team that is called for an offensive foul has to turn the ball over to the other team. They lose a chance to score, and even worse, they give their opponent another chance to put points on the board. Sometimes when a team commits a foul their opponent gets to go to the free throw line. This happens when a player is fouled as he is shooting or when the team that commits the foul is in the penalty.

Fouls can be bad for individual players because a player fouls out of a game after collecting five or six fouls. In high school and college, players get six fouls; in professional play, they only get five. If you foul out, you won't be able to help your team on the court at the end of the game when it might matter the most. Making two or three mistakes early in a game can get you in what is called foul trouble, and your coach might have you sit on the bench so you won't foul out. The best plan is to not foul, to play smart.

WORDS TO KNOW

Fake

A fake is when a player simulates a shot or a move to the basket to get his opponent to think he is going to do one thing, but then he does something else. The fake, if done well, gets the defender off balance or even out of the way and can often draw a foul.

Turnover

The other team gets possession of the ball. Turnovers happen for a number of reasons. If you step out of bounds or commit a foul, you'll have to turn the ball over. Your opponent can also steal the ball from you or intercept a pass. Players and teams who have good fundamentals often commit fewer turnovers.

Rebounding

When you gain possession of the basketball after a missed shot or free throw, you have rebounded the ball. It's one of the most important aspects of the game because most possessions end when a team misses a shot and there is a rebound. There are two kinds of rebounds: offensive and defensive.

Offense and Defense

The offensive rebound comes when your team shoots and you or a teammate get the ball back. The defensive rebound comes when the opponent has shot the ball at the basket and missed and your team recovers the ball. The majority of rebounds go to the defensive side because the defenders usually have better position around the basket as they defend it.

Being a Good Rebounder

Rebounding is a part of the game that affects you both offensively and defensively. If you let the opposing team shoot and miss and get the ball again, they have another chance to put points on the board. If your team misses a shot and does not get the rebound, you've lost an opportunity to score. However, if you get the offensive rebound, you give your team another chance to score.

Rebounding is about body position and tenacity. Six-foot-four forward Charles Barkley averaged more rebounds for his career than seven-foot-one center Shaquille O'Neal has. While centers do get a lot of the rebounds because they are tall, they still need to get in the right position. A center that stands away from the basket or behind two offensive players who are closer to the rim probably won't get a rebound, no matter how tall she is. Besides, some of the best rebounders in the pro and college games have been players of only average basketball height. They end up with more rebounds by positioning themselves correctly and never giving up.

WORDS TO KNOW

In the penalty
After a team has committed a certain number of fouls—four in one quarter in the professional leagues, seven in one half for college-level basketball—their opponent gets to shoot free throws for every subsequent foul for the rest of the quarter or half.

Technical foul
A referee can call a technical foul on a player or coach for unsportsmanlike conduct. A second technical foul results in ejection. Technical fouls can also be called for, well, technical reasons, such as trying to call a timeout when a team doesn't have any left. The penalty for drawing a technical foul varies by league.

Flagrant foul
A flagrant foul is called for a particularly hard foul that either injured a player or could have caused a serious injury. If a referee thinks the player committed a flagrant foul on purpose, that player can be thrown out of the game. The opposing team goes to the free throw line and gets to keep possession of the ball once play resumes.

If you are on the offensive end, your focus should be on getting in front of the defenders, closer to the rim but far enough away from it to get the ball if the shot misses. You don't want to be right under the rim because the only way you will get the ball is if it goes through the hoop, and in that case your team has scored and there's no rebound to be gotten! You want to be where you think the ball is likely to come down, never under the basket.

How to Rebound

The players who get the rebounds either don't have to jump or don't have to jump very high because they are in the right place and the ball actually seems to find them. You must believe that the ball is yours and you are going to do what it takes—within the rules, of course—to get it. That starts with proper positioning near the basket. Offensive rebounds are harder to get because the team on defense usually has two or three players gathered around the basket who are ready to stop you if you try to drive the lane, which means dribbling toward the basket on through the area on either side of the free throw area. If you are on the offensive end and you see a teammate taking a shot, try to get around your defender, especially if she has given up guarding you, and move into the best position to secure a possible rebound.

What to Do with Your Rebound

Once you get a rebound, bring the ball down close to your chest with your elbows out to each side, which will help you keep your balance and keep the ball from being knocked away or stolen from you. If it is an offensive rebound, you might want to jump right back up to try to score again or pivot and look to pass. If you are in a crowd and can dribble out, you can do that and pass it so your team can set up another play.

Defensive rebounds are really important to your team. If a team gets three or four rebounds every time they have the

TIP-IN

The best rebounding team in NBA history was the 1959–1960 Boston Celtics, who averaged 71.5 rebounds per game. The team to average the fewest rebounds per game was the 1995–1996 Cleveland Cavaliers, who averaged 35.6 rebounds per game.

ball, there's a good chance they'll score every time. You want to give them one chance, if that; you have to protect the basket. Even if you are guarding the player who shoots, you can help with rebounding. When a player shoots the ball, you should move into position to get a rebound or box out your opponent—keeping a player from getting between you and the basket to get a rebound.

You can never work too hard at rebounding. You also want to work smart when getting the proper position. If you don't get the rebound, don't make your situation worse by fouling the player who did get the rebound. Instead, immediately refocus and commit to playing great defense and then double your awareness and effort to get the next rebound.

Fun Games to Sharpen Your Skills

These games are a great way to really hone in on specific basketball skills. You can play some of them by yourself; others work better if you have two, three, four, or more!

H-O-R-S-E

Want to sharpen your skills with a friend? One classic game is H-O-R-S-E, a shot-making game of skill. You take a shot from anywhere on the court. If you make it, your opponent has to make a shot from the same place. If they miss, they get the letter H. Keep playing until one of you ends up with five letters—H-O-R-S-E—at which point that player has lost.

You can do long shots, close shots, free throws, layups, and even trick shots. If you're just beginning or are playing on a team, it's always better to get good at making the standard shots first. If you can make baskets from a variety of places, your coach and teammates can count on you to score a basket if they get the ball to you.

FUN FACTS

If you are just starting basketball or think H-O-R-S-E is going to take too long, a popular shorter version of the game is P-I-G. But you can also use longer words, too, if you really want to work on your shooting—and spelling—skills!

Take a Trip Around the World

Another game is Around the World. This works best if you play it with one or two others. Start by making a layup, then backing up with two or three shots on the hash marks of the key. The hash marks denotes where players stand during free throws, with the first spot reserved for the players from the defending team, and then alternating with offensive and defensive players. There are spots for four players on each side of the free throw area. To continue doing this drill, once you shoot a free throw, you go to the top of the key to make a three pointer before closing in toward the hoop again by making shots from the hash marks on the other side of the key. To finish, you make a layup.

Sound too easy? Make it harder by giving yourself only two chances to make a shot from a given place. For example, if you get to the free throw line and miss, you freeze there while your opponent has a turn. When it's your turn again, a missed shot means you give the ball to your friend; on your next turn, you have start over at the beginning. The farther you are "around the world," the more devastating the miss.

Knockout or Bump

This game requires two balls and as many players as you can get together. Players line up in a single-file line at any spot on the floor, usually at the foul line or behind the three-point arc. The first two in line each have a ball. The object is to make a shot before the player in front of you makes his.

The first player in line shoots. The second person in line with the ball can shoot only after the player in front releases the ball. If the second player shoots the ball and makes her shot before the player in front of her, then the first player is out.

If a player misses his shot, he is able to rebound and try to put it back in from anywhere on the court. If the first shooter makes her basket first, she passes the ball to the next player in line so he can try to make a basket before the player in front of him. Proceed until there is only one player left.

Twenty-One

The game is played to 21 points. You receive one point for a free throw, two points from inside the three-point line, and three points from behind the three-point line. You can play the game with two or more players.

One player starts with the ball; the others position themselves to try to grab a rebound. The player with the ball shoots a free throw. If she makes it, she gets one point and gets the ball back for another free throw. If she makes the second free throw, she racks up another point and gets possession of the ball at the top of the key. She can make a shot from anywhere on the court, but now the other players can play defense. If she makes the shot, she earns more points and goes back to the free throw line to start the cycle again.

If a player misses a free throw, the ball is considered live, and any player can rebound it. Whoever comes away with the ball has to dribble it past the three-point line before trying to make a shot. If he makes it, it's his turn to go to the free throw line. The first player to get twenty-one points is the winner.

PLAY BALL

Netball is a game that is very similar to basketball but was created just for girls and women to play. How many words can you make out of the letters in N E T B A L L?

Lists of Lists

Basketball fans love lists and statistics. These "Lists of 10" have become scattered. Do you know where they should go? Figure out what group they belong to and write the group number on the line next to the word.

GROUP 1: Sports with the letter B in them
GROUP 2: Sports equipment
GROUP 3: Cities that have hosted the Olympics
GROUP 4: Sports where you don't kick a ball

snowboarding ____

ballooning ____

Innsbruck ____

shoulder pads ____

skip rope ____

Nagano ____

water polo ____

golf ____

badminton ____

catcher's mitt ____

wrist guard ____

racquetball ____

handball ____

helmet ____

knee pads ____

basketball ____

baseball bat ____

ski pole ____

Atlanta ____

Beijing ____

lacrosse ____

Turin ____

Los Angeles ____

bungee jumping ____

squash ____

swimming ____

ultimate Frisbee ____

goggles ____

T-ball ____

tennis ____

Barcelona ____

powerboating ____

flippers ____

Sydney ____

Seoul ____

diving ____

Calgary ____

skiing ____

baseball ____

hockey ____

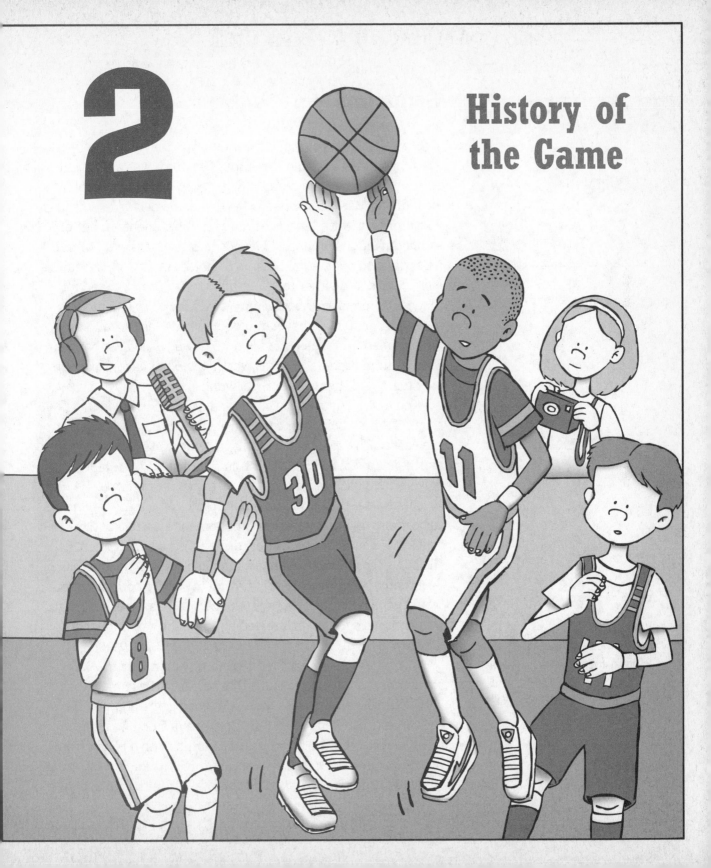

2

History of the Game

Game On!

Basketball was actually invented by a Canadian teaching in New England. Dr. James Naismith was a physical education teacher and student at a YMCA Training School in Springfield, Massachusetts, in 1891 when he decided he needed to come up with an activity to keep his students in better shape during the long, cold New England winters. He wanted an activity to do in a gymnasium. Though many of his ideas were considered either too physically rough or not suited for indoors (some involved tackling), James took a peach basket and nailed it 10 feet above an indoor track. "Basket ball," as James called it, was born. A soccer ball was used to shoot baskets. At first, each basket was worth one point each, so whichever team had the most baskets won.

The first game was played in January 1892. It ended in a 1-0 score. The only point came from a shot taken 25 feet away from the basket. The court was roughly half the size of the present-day standard court. By 1898, the standard rule was that five players from each team could be on the court at a time.

Since a peach basket had a bottom in it, the ball would have to be manually removed each time someone made a basket. To make it easier, James had a hole drilled through the bottom of the basket so a rod could be used to push the ball up and out. Eventually, he figured out that having the entire bottom cut out would work better, though by 1906 the sport had grown so fast that rims with nets were created to shape the game much as it is today.

In James's diaries, recovered by family members in 2006, many were astonished to learn that he based the game of basketball largely on the rules for a childhood game popular in the 1800s called "Duck and Run," in which a stone was placed on an elevated object, usually a tree stump, with a player from one team guarding it. Players would throw "ducks" (rocks) at the stone to try and knock it off the pedestal. Once the stone was

James never played basketball in college—because he had not invented it yet. However, he was a standout athlete at Canada's McGill College as a lacrosse and football player and as a gymnast.

Duck on a Rock

Duck on a Rock was the game that inspired the modern game of basketball. Here are the rules:

One player guards the platform (usually a tree stump or large stone), which has a smaller stone sitting on top of it. The smaller stone is called a drake. The other players toss their stones (known as ducks) at the drake to knock it off. Once the drake is knocked off, players run to retrieve their ducks. If a player is tagged before returning to the throwing line, he becomes the guard. Before the guard tags anyone, she has to pick up a duck at her feet and put the drake back on the platform. Have fun, but be careful how you toss the stones!

No Law of the Jungle

Why are there no fair sports players in the jungle?

Because of all the cheetahs!

successfully knocked off, the players would run to try to pick up their ducks, but if they were tagged before returning successfully behind the throwing line, they were "it" and had to guard the stone.

Naismith's Rules

James came up with 13 original rules for his game of basket ball. Some of these have changed since his teams first started playing the game.

1. **Original rule:** Players may throw the ball in any direction using one or both hands.
   Now: That's still true, but once the offensive team brings the ball past half-court, the ball cannot be passed into the backcourt.

2. **Original rule:** Players may touch the ball to make it go in any direction, but may not use fists.
   Now: Still true, but the fist rule has been relaxed. Touch passes do not involve using the fist and even blocked shots seldom involve a fist.

3. **Original rule:** Players cannot run with the ball. When you catch the ball, you must stop and throw the ball from that spot. You are allowed a few steps to slow down if you are running when you catch the ball.
   Now: Players cannot hold the ball and run with it, but they are allowed to dribble it up and down the court. A player who holds on to the ball while he runs is called for traveling and the ball is turned over to the other team. However, if a player is streaking toward the basket, catches the ball at a dead run, and only has a step or two until he shoots it, he can usually get away without dribbling it,

TIP-IN

James's students used a soccer ball for the first basketball games. To grip the ball better, they would rub coal dust on their hands.

though many purists say this should not be allowed.

4. **Original rule:** Players must hold the ball with their hands; the arms and body cannot be used to hold the ball.
Now: The ball can only be held in the hands or the arms.

5. **Original rule:** Players are not allowed to shoulder, hold, push, trip, or hit each other. The first time a player is called for illegal behavior, it counts as a foul. The second time, the player cannot play until the next basket is scored. If a player meant to injure an opponent, he is ejected from the game and no one is allowed to take his place on the court.
Now: The penalties have changed. Five or six fouls are required to foul out. An intentional or flagrant foul can cause a player to be ejected from the game, though he can be replaced on the floor.

6. **Original rule:** Striking the ball with a fist or breaking rules 3, 4, or 5 counts as a foul.
Now: Players can do touch passes and be creative with passes.

7. **Original rule:** If one side racks up three fouls in a row, the other team is awarded a basket.
Now: This is no longer the case. If a team commits a certain number of fouls, their opponent gets to shoot free throws for each subsequent foul.

8. **Original rule:** A goal is made when the ball is thrown into the basket and stays there. If an opponent moves the basket to prevent a ball from going in, it counts as a goal.
Now: The original basket did not have a hole in it, which is why James wrote that the ball had to stay in the basket to count as a goal. This obviously isn't the case anymore. A goal—now called a basket—is when the ball goes through

★ FUN FACTS ★

While James brought the game of basketball into existence, he remains the only basketball coach ever at the University of Kansas to have a losing career record. He stepped down with a career mark of 55-60.

the net. James's original rule does cover what came to be known as goaltending, meaning the ball cannot be touched when it is on the rim and headed into the basket.

9. **Original rule:** A ball that goes out of bounds can be thrown back onto the court by the player who touches it first. If two players get to the ball at the same time, the umpire throws the ball back onto the court. A player has five seconds to throw the ball; if she goes over, the other team gets the ball. A foul is called if either side delays the game.
Now: Instead of letting everyone scramble for the ball, the current rule states that the team that touched the ball last before it went out of bounds loses possession of the ball. The five-second rule is still in effect. All in-bounds passes must be made within five seconds or the other team gets the ball out of bounds. Also, whenever a player has the ball on the court, he must pass, shoot, or dribble the ball within five seconds or the ball is turned over to the other team.

10. **Original rule:** The umpire calls fouls and keeps track of how many fouls have been made. He can throw players out of the game according to Rule 5.
Now: Most levels of basketball have two or even three referees, and it takes five or six fouls for a player to foul out of a game. The officials do still have the power to eject a player from the game for a flagrant foul.

11. **Original rule:** The referee is in charge of deciding the following areas: when the ball is in play, whether it is in bounds, which side has possession, whether a basket has been made. The referee is also in charge of the game clock and keeping score.
Now: Referees and officials still keep track of all of this. There are officials whose entire job is to keep track of the time and the score of the game, so the referees on the

TIP-IN

When you are guarding the player who is passing the ball in-bounds, have your hands up and watch her eyes—not the ball—so you can see where she is looking to pass the ball. This way, you can try to block that area or deflect the ball.

floor can concentrate on other things.

12. **Original rule:** The game is made up of two 15-minute halves with a five-minute halftime.

Now: The college game has halves and the NBA has quarters. The length of the game varies depending on the level of the game—YMCA, college, professional, or another level. The NBA has four 12-minute quarters and college has two 20-minute halves.

13. **Original rule:** The team that makes the most goals wins the game. If the game ends in a tie, the team captains can decide whether to continue the game until another goal is made.

Now: The team with the most points wins. There is no sudden-death overtime where the team that shoots the first basket wins. Instead, teams play an overtime period, and the team with the most points at the end of overtime wins.

★ **FUN FACTS** ★

Basketball became a medal event at the 1936 Summer Olympics in Berlin, Germany. James was there to hand out the first basketball gold medal—to the United States. He also presented the silver medal to his native Canada and the bronze to Mexico.

Lucky 13

Some people think 13 is an unlucky number, but it wasn't for James Naismith. His 13 rules worked very well for him. Here are some other things that are considered unlucky. Can you spot all 5?

The BBA—The Beginning of the NBA

At the Hotel Commodore in New York on June 6, 1946, a group of basketball team owners met to talk about a league—the Basketball Association of America—they hoped to start. These were men who controlled the sports and entertainment arenas in big cities; today's owners are mostly businessmen.

With World War II over, the owners felt Americans were ready to spend dollars on entertainment and sports. College basketball was already an incredible success, and the owners hoped they could convince some of the college stars to be part of a professional league. On June 11, two conferences were formed: the Western Conference, made up of the Pittsburgh Ironmen, Chicago Stags, Detroit Falcons, St. Louis Bombers, and Cleveland Rebels; and the Eastern Conference, made up of the Boston Celtics, Philadelphia Warriors, Providence Steamrollers, Washington Capitols, New York Knickerbockers, and Toronto Huskies.

The first game was scheduled for November 1, just five months away, and the rules were based largely on those from the college game. However, rather than play two halves, the pro league decided to go with four 12-minute quarters. With timeouts, halftimes, and other time stoppages, the evening entertainment would stretch to two hours, something owners felt was important to their customers. Though zone defenses were prevalent in college, the owners decided that no zone defense would be allowed for at least the first year. They were afraid the zone defense would slow down the game, so they allowed only man-to-man defense.

To get local fans and to keep travel costs down, teams selected players from local colleges. Providence took players from Rhode Island colleges, Knicks' players came from New York, and Pittsburgh looked for players within a 100-mile radius of the city. The only exception was Toronto, which had just one Canadian player among its mostly American roster. The contracts were very modest compared to the multimillion dollar deals of today.

The first professional basketball game was played in Canada in 1946. The Toronto Huskies hosted the New York Knickerbockers at Maple Leaf Gardens, home of the famous Canadian hockey team the Toronto Maple Leafs.

The opening game had 7,090 fans, and the Knicks won an exciting 68-66 contest. There was no 24-second shot clock, so teams were in no hurry to score, which explains the low point total compared to today's NBA game.

A Competing League

In 1967, the American Basketball Association (ABA) was founded. Like the NBA, it had an Eastern Conference and a Western Conference. The Eastern Conference was made up of the Pittsburgh Pipers, Minnesota Muskies, Indiana Pacers, Kentucky Colonels, and New Jersey Americans. The Western

TIP-IN

Three of the most famous sports arenas were commonly called the Garden. The first basketball game was played in Toronto's hockey rink, Maple Leaf Gardens, but NBA fans probably know the current New York Knicks home is Madison Square Garden. The Celtics played in the Boston Garden, which was demolished in 1997 and replaced by the TD Garden.

WORDS TO KNOW

Shot clock
The shot clock for college and pro games is centered on top of the backboard. It starts when a team takes position of the ball and it is not reset until the ball hits the rim on a shot attempt or the clock winds down to zero.

★ FUN FACTS ★

The original BBA didn't look much like today's NBA. New teams have been created and old teams have folded. Franchises moved from city to city, sometimes changing their names. Most recently, in 2008, the Seattle SuperSonics moved across the country to become the Oklahoma City Thunder.

★ FUN FACTS ★

The ABA was easily recognizable in newspaper photos or TV highlights because the basketball was red, white, and blue. One of the more popular fan promotions was ball night. A set number of fans received a ball when they bought a ticket and entered the arena for the game that night.

conference was made up of the New Orleans Buccaneers, Dallas Chaparrals, Denver Rockets, Houston Mavericks, Anaheim Amigos, and Oakland Oaks. The ABA was always struggling financially compared to the NBA. The NBA invited the ABA to join together, which they did in 1976. This made the ABA franchises more valuable and guaranteed the teams would survive.

CURRENT NBA TEAMS	
Eastern Conference	
Atlantic Division	Boston Celtics • Toronto Raptors • Philadelphia 76ers • New Jersey Nets • New York Knicks
Central Division	Detroit Pistons • Cleveland Cavaliers • Indiana Pacers • Chicago Bulls • Milwaukee Bucks
Southeast Division	Orlando Magic • Washington Wizards • Atlanta Hawks • Charlotte Bobcats • Miami Heat
Western Conference	
Northwest Division	Utah Jazz • Denver Nuggets • Portland Trail Blazers • Minnesota Timberwolves • Oklahoma City Thunder
Pacific Division	L.A. Lakers • Phoenix Suns • Golden State Warriors • Sacramento Kings • L.A. Clippers
Southwest Division	New Orleans Hornets • San Antonio Spurs • Houston Rockets • Dallas Mavericks • Memphis Grizzlies

Olympic Dream Teams

The Olympics changed forever when professional athletes were allowed to represent their countries. Previously, the Olympic Games had been reserved for amateurs, but the rules changed for the 1992 Olympic Games in Barcelona, when professional athletes were allowed to compete.

Do What Coach Says

These 12 players need a makeover. The coach says they can join the team if they dress the way he likes. Look at the following statements and figure out who will be on the team. What fraction of the 12 players will make the cut?

- The players with beards will get on the team.

- The players with feathers in their hats won't get on the team.

- The players with glasses will get on the team.

- The players with polka dots on their shirts will not get on the team.

Around the World

After inventing the game of basketball, Canadian doctor James Naismith lived to see it spread across the globe with the help of the YMCA.

1992 Dream Team

The United States chose 12 of the NBA's best athletes to compete in Olympic men's basketball. Ten of the players were later voted among the 50 Greatest Players in NBA History for the NBA's 50th anniversary in 1996. Michael Jordan, Earvin "Magic" Johnson, Larry Bird, Clyde Drexler, Patrick Ewing, David Robinson, John Stockton, Karl Malone, Charles Barkley, Scottie Pippen, Chris Mullin, and Christian Laettner all starred on the team. Chuck Daly, the Hall of Fame coach who had engineered the Detroit Pistons' back-to-back NBA championship wins in 1989 and 1990, helmed the Dream Team.

The 1992 Dream Team cruised to a 6-0 record in qualifying play in Barcelona. Even in the quarterfinals, Chris scored a team-leading 21 points to help eliminate Puerto Rico 115-77. The semifinals saw a 51-point U.S. win over Lithuania, and nine Americans scored in double figures. In the gold medal game, the United States beat Croatia by 32 points—and though the game was a blowout, it was the closest score of any game for the United States.

1996 Olympics: Atlanta, Georgia

The United States hosted the 1996 Olympics, so a new Dream Team had a chance to compete on their home soil. Charles, Karl, John, Scottie, and Davis were joined by Shaquille O'Neal, Reggie Miller, Hakeem Olajuwon, Gary Payton, Mitch Richmond, Anfernee Hardaway, and Grant Hill. Coached by Hall of Famer Lenny Wilkens, the Americans were once again head and shoulders above the rest. The United States pounded Yugoslavia in the gold medal game 95-69.

2000 Olympics: Sydney, Australia

By 2000, the NBA had more international players among its ranks than ever before, and leagues in other countries were beginning to gain strength. Though the U.S. team had a lot

★ **FUN FACTS** ★

The Dream Team's margin of victory was much smaller in 1996 than in 1992. In 1992, the Dream Team won its games by an average of 44 points. It won its closest game—the gold medal game against Croatia—by 32 points. Compare that to 1996, when the Americans' average margin of victory was 32.3 points.

of talent, it was not as dominant as past Dream Teams. Gary returned as the sole Olympic veteran. He was joined by Alonzo Mourning, Kevin Garnett, Vince Carter, Allan Houston, Vin Baker, Antonio McDyess, Steve Smith, Ray Allen, Jason Kidd, Shareef Abdur-Rahim, and Tim Hardaway. Though the 2000 U.S. team was undefeated, five of the eight games were decided by a margin of 15 or fewer points. The American's closest call came in the semifinals, when they squeaked by Lithuania 85-83. They won the gold medal by beating France 85-75.

2004 Olympics: Athens, Greece

In 2004, the Dream Team had the ultimate team player in NBA star Tim Duncan, but many of his teammates were known more for individual talent than team championships. Hall of Fame coach Larry Brown commanded a team full of young players. Promising up-and-coming stars LeBron James, Carmelo Anthony, Dwyane Wade, Carlos Boozer, Richard Jefferson, Amare Stoudemire, and Emeka Okafor joined NBA

TIP-IN

Why don't the best NBA players always win gold medals at the Olympics? Because fundamentals and defense are the keys to international basketball. Also, many teams from other countries play together year-round, while the NBA players practice on the same team for only a few weeks to get ready for the Olympics.

Inflated Basketball

The first time basketball players made money was in 1896. The team couldn't play in their usual space, so they rented a hall, charged admission, and split the profits. They each got $15. That would be the equivalent of $375 today! The amounts on the balls are in 1896 dollars. If $1 is worth 25 times what it was in 1896, how much would the items cost today?

$20

$27

$32

$50

veterans Tim Duncan, Allen Iverson, Stephon Marbury, Shawn Marion, and Lamar Odom. But the team never really came together.

Puerto Rico beat the Dream Team soundly, 92-73, in the opening game of the Olympics. The United States won close games with Greece and Australia but fell to Lithuania in its fourth game. An easy win over Angola got the U.S. into the medal round, and in the quarterfinals the Dream Team beat Spain 102-94. But in the semifinals, Argentina, a team that focused on playing fundamentally sound team basketball and good defense, beat the U.S. 89-81, eliminating the United States from gold medal competition. The Americans defeated Lithuania in the third-place game to win the bronze medal.

2008 Redeem Team

For the 2008 Olympics in Beijing, China, the United States assembled a team with talent the likes of which hadn't been seen since the original 1992 Dream Team. Dubbed the Redeem Team, its players promised to return to the fundamentals that had made the United States so dominant in the past.

James, Wade, Anthony, and Boozer returned, joined by Chris Bosh, Kobe Bryant, Dwight Howard, Jason Kidd, Chris Paul, Tayshaun Prince, Michael Redd, and Deron Williams. Under the direction of Mike Krzyzewski, Duke's legendary Hall of Fame coach, the Redeem Team did exactly what it set out to do. It won every game by double digits, beating Spain in the gold medal game 118-107, and proved that the United States was once again the team to beat.

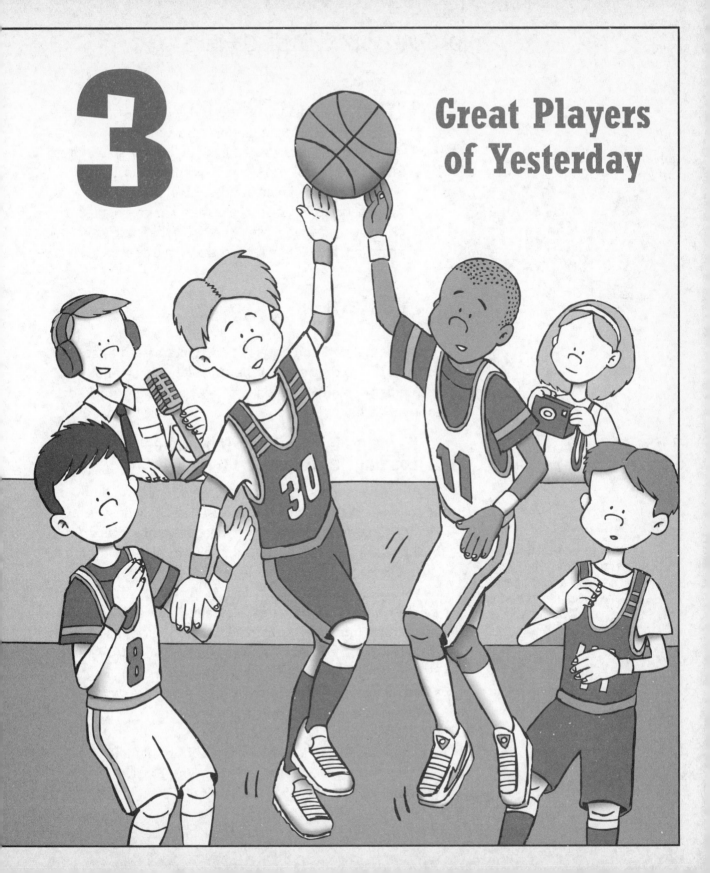

3

Great Players
of Yesterday

The NBA has had many great players since it was started in 1946. One of the fun things for fans to do is argue about who was better, and they will often cite statistics or championships to bolster their argument. Though this is by no means a complete list (the Hall of Fame chapter has more), here are several of the players who contributed to the league's amazing history and built the foundation upon which millions of fans support the league every year.

Centers

Center is a very dominant position. Centers need to be big but agile so they can get the ball, block shots, and grab rebounds before their opponents. They're not usually known for their ability to hit shots, but a few are able to do it all.

Kareem Abdul-Jabbar: Milwaukee Bucks, Los Angeles Lakers

Like Lakers modern-day great Kobe Bryant, Kareem Abdul-Jabbar was not drafted by the Lakers. Kareem, who was born Ferdinand Lewis Alcindor but changed his name, was drafted by the Milwaukee Bucks as the first pick in the 1969 draft after a great career at UCLA under legendary coach John Wooden. He won three straight collegiate championships (freshmen were not allowed to play then). Kareem, who was rookie of the year, played until age 42 and holds records for points scored, shots blocked, most seasons played, most NBA Most Valuable Player Awards (6), and the most all-star games (18). He was able to change the game because even though he was over seven feet tall, he was still graceful and quick. Defenders were powerless to stop his "Sky Hook" shot.

Kareem helped his teams win six NBA Championships and was chosen to both the 35th and 50th Anniversary All-

★ FUN FACTS ★

Kareem gained good reviews for his comedic role in the classic movie *Airplane!,* in which he made several humorous references about playing defense and quips about former teammates.

Time Teams. A lot of people know Kareem from his championships with the Lakers later in his career, when he played with Magic Johnson. Kareem actually won an NBA title in his second year in the league with the Milwaukee Bucks playing with his talented point-guard teammate Oscar Robertson. Kareem was named NBA finals MVP in that series.

Kareem was traded to the Los Angeles Lakers in 1975 and won another NBA Most Valuable Player Award that season. The Lakers became great again and won nine division titles in Kareem's final 10 years, during which Kareem helped lead the Lakers to five NBA Championship titles.

KAREEM ABDUL-JABBAR

Points	Rebounds	Assists
24.6	11.2	3.6

Willis Reed, New York Knicks

The image of Willis Reed limping out to lead his New York Knicks to the NBA Championship in Game 7 of the 1970 NBA Finals is among the most memorable in league history to many fans, especially those in New York. Willis had dominated the series. The 6 foot, 10 inch, 245-pound Willis had lit up the Los Angeles Lakers for 37 points in Game 1 of the Finals, 29 in Game 2, 38 in Game 3, and 23 in Game 4, and averaged 15 rebounds a game. But early in the series, his thigh was injured with a deep bruise that many feared would keep him out of the rest of the series.

The Knicks were hammered by the Lakers in Game 6, and no one knew if Willis would be able to play in Game 7. He gamely limped onto the court and fired up his teammates by out-jumping Wilt Chamberlain for the jump ball to start the game, and then scored the game's first basket. Though he didn't score again, Willis's teammates rode that momentum

★ FUN FACTS ★

Kareem changed his name in 1971 after converting from Catholicism to Islam. Kareem Abdul-Jabbar means "powerful, noble servant." He was certainly powerful on the court.

TIP-IN

Willis also knew how to come up big as an executive with the New Jersey Nets. He lured Detroit's championship-winning coach, Chuck Daly, to come coach the Nets for two years in the early 1990s.

to a 29-point lead at one point in support of Willis and rolled to the NBA Championship. Willis was MVP in 1970 and went on to help lead the Knicks to a title in 1973.

WILLIS REED

Points	Rebounds	Assists
18.7	12.9	1.8

George Mikan: Chicago, Minneapolis

The first real big man to dominate the professional game, 6 foot, 10 inch George Mikan averaged more than 23 points and more than 13 rebounds a game for his career. George played college basketball for DePaul, where he led his team to the NIT title and was twice National College Player of the Year. He started out by playing one year for the Chicago American Gears in the National Basketball League (NBL), leading his team to the league title, before joining the NBL's Minneapolis Lakers. Along with teammate Jim Pollard, he led Minneapolis to the NBL title, George's second in two years.

After that season, Minneapolis was among the NBL franchises that defected to the BAA. In 1949, George led the Lakers to the championship despite suffering a broken wrist halfway through the finals. The BAA and NBL fully merged the following year to create the NBA, and teams led by George won NBA titles in 1950, 1952, 1953, and 1954, the first dynasty of the league.

★ FUN FACTS ★

Not only did George revolutionize the game for big men, he was known for wearing very large glasses and being able to shoot the ball with either hand, which made it even harder for players to guard him.

GEORGE MIKAN

Points	Rebounds	Assists
23.1	13.4	2.8

Court Count

This game has gotten completely out of hand! There are 2 players on the court who don't belong. Can you spot them?

The Fingers of One Hand

On a 10-player team, only 5 players are allowed on the court at any one time.

Hakeem Olajuwon: Houston Rockets

Hakeem "The Dream" Olajuwon led the Houston Rockets to their first two titles in NBA history. In 1993–1994, he had a dream season when he won the league Most Valuable Player Award and the NBA Finals MVP honor while leading Houston to its first NBA championship. During the season Hakeem averaged 33 points a game in the playoffs to lead Houston to its second NBA title. He followed that up with a spot on the 1996 U.S. Olympic Dream Team, which won a gold medal in Atlanta.

For his size, Hakeem had surprising agility and a soft touch shooting the basketball and he developed a wide array of offensive shots, including spin moves and fade-away jump shots that defenders could find no way to stop. He averaged 26 points or more per game for four seasons in a row. He was also a defensive force, winning the Defensive Player of the Year award in 1993.

HAKEEM OLAJUWON

Points	Rebounds	Assists
21.8	11.1	2.5

Bill Russell: Boston Celtics

As a college player at San Francisco, Bill Russell led his team to two NCAA championships—in 1955 and 1956—though he was forced to miss the final four games of the 1956 NCAA tournament because his college eligibility had expired. Bill still made an important appearance in a championship game in 1956, when he led the U.S. Olympic Basketball Team to a gold medal at the Olympics in Melbourne, Australia.

Bill almost did not end up a Boston Celtics player, but NBA coach and general manager Red Auerbach wanted Bill so badly that he traded for the second pick in the draft to get him. Bill was a defensive power, changing the game of basketball by blocking shots. He also had 21,620 rebounds during his career, an average of 22.5 rebounds a game, a huge number that hasn't been matched since. Bill led the league in rebounding four times. He once had 51 rebounds in a single game; twice had 49 rebounds in a game. But above all, Bill was regarded as the ultimate team player and a winner. He led the Celtics to 11 NBA Championships in his 13 seasons. Bill is regarded as the most dominant big man in the game, and only Michael Jordan is referred to more often as the game's greatest player. Bill was no 7-foot giant, either; he was 6 feet 9 inches tall.

In the NBA, Bill's greatest foe was Wilt Chamberlain, who put up great offensive numbers, but Bill's team-first attitude led to far more championships than Wilt would ever attain.

TIP-IN

Bill was a diamond in the rough when he started playing basketball, and his fundamentals were so weak that he was almost cut from his high school team as a sophomore. A coach helped him learn how to properly play the game. Hard work took care of the rest, and by his junior year Bill was the best player on the team.

BILL RUSSELL

Points	Rebounds	Assists
15.1	22.5	4.3

Wilt Chamberlain: Philadelphia, San Francisco, Los Angeles

Wilt "The Stilt" Chamberlain was seen as the most powerful offensive player in the game. He was a dominant figure at 7 feet 1 inch tall and 300 pounds. Wilt left the game with several NBA records. He was the only player to score 4,000 points in a season. He scored 100 points for the Philadelphia Warriors in a victory against the Knicks in 1962. He also set an NBA record with 55 rebounds in one game. His offensive numbers were hard to comprehend; Wilt averaged 50.4 points during the 1961–1962 season. His 31,419 points were a record at the time of retirement, though he was later passed by Kareem Abdul-Jabbar, Karl Malone, and Michael Jordan.

Wilt was also a defensive force, leading the league in

rebounding 11 of the 14 seasons he played. He could also pass, leading the league in assists in 1967–1968. He was constantly double-teamed and even triple-teamed, and the NBA itself had to change some of the rules to negate Wilt's dominance. Because of Wilt, the NBA came up with the offensive goaltending rule. Once a ball has reached the top of its arc and is headed down into the basket, it is illegal to tip the ball in. Rule changes also widened the lane and made inbounding the basketball more structured to keep Wilt from controlling the entire game. Wilt used to shoot free throws by jumping from the free throw line and dropping the ball into the hoop until the league changed the rule to say that players must remain behind the foul line.

WILT CHAMBERLAIN

Points	Rebounds	Assists
30.1	22.9	4.4

Bill Walton: Portland, San Diego, Boston

Bill Walton was supposed to be the next big thing in the NBA when he came out of UCLA, but the big man struggled with injuries. Despite those injuries, he won an NBA title and an NBA MVP award in his first four years with the Portland Trail Blazers. He averaged nearly 18 points and more than 13 rebounds a game during his final three years in Portland. His numbers declined for the following three years after he was traded to San Diego. He was rescued by Boston and became a key role player on Boston's run to its league championship in 1986, a season in which Bill came off the bench and won the NBA's Sixth Man Award. A chronically broken foot bone kept him injured off and on throughout his career, but he still became a Hall of Famer and was selected as one of the NBA's top 50 players of all time.

BILL WALTON

Points	Rebounds	Assists
13.3	10.5	3.4

Patrick Ewing: New York Knicks, Seattle, Orlando

Though he bounced around the final couple of seasons in the league after an Achilles tendon injury effectively ended his career, Patrick Ewing will always be remembered for his dominant years as the New York Knicks's prototypical 7-foot center. He was also among the better shooting centers in the game and retired as the Knicks's all-time scoring and rebound leader. Patrick also helped lead the United States to a pair of Olympic gold medals in 1992 and 1996.

Unfortunately, Patrick was never able to deliver a championship to New York, although he came close. He took his team to the NBA Finals in 1984, where they lost to the Houston Rockets.

PATRICK EWING

Points	Rebounds	Assists
21.0	9.8	1.9

David Robinson: San Antonio Spurs

David Robinson came out of the Navy, earned the nickname "The Admiral," and steered his Spurs to two NBA Championships in 1999 and 2003. He was also Defensive Player of the Year in 1992 and NBA MVP in 1995. At 7 feet 1 inch, David was tall, but he was lean and in such good shape that he rarely tired and was among the most athletic centers ever to play the game. David was actually in the latter stages

★ **FUN FACTS** ★

Patrick is another international player who starred as center. Originally from Jamaica, Patrick was better at cricket and soccer than he was at basketball when he was young.

of his career when he finally won his NBA championships. Tim Duncan, who like David carried himself with dignity and was considered the consummate teammate, joined the team and turned the Spurs from good to great. David also competed in three Olympic Games and helped the United States win two medals, in 1992 and 1996.

DAVID ROBINSON

Points	Rebounds	Assists
21.1	10.6	2.5

Guards

The guard is the quarterback of the offense. The point guard sets up the plays and makes a lot of the key passes, and the shooting guard has a lot of pressure to shoot effectively from the outside and help rebound. These are faster players than the forwards and centers, so they must hurry back on defense. On defense, they do much more running around guarding players than the taller players, who cover a smaller area nearer the basketball hoop.

Michael Jordan: Chicago, Washington

Ask almost anyone who the best NBA player of all time was, and Michael Jordan is usually the first name mentioned. Michael was, above all else, a dominant player and a winner. After he scored 63 points in a playoff game against Larry Bird's Celtics in his second year, Bird described what he had seen as "God disguised as Michael Jordan." The 6 foot 5 inch Michael was a five-time NBA MVP who redefined the game offensively. He scored seemingly at will, defied gravity with a variety of dunks, and—perhaps most importantly—made all the players around him better. Michael and his teammates in the Chicago Bulls won six NBA titles. Nike built its basketball shoe—the Air Jordan—for Michael. As a player, Michael had few peers; he was too tall for a guard to defend but too fast and too good of a shooter for a forward to try to stop.

A perennial all-star and MVP, the only question each year often seemed to be who Michael's Chicago Bulls would see in the NBA finals. The Bulls dynasty was built entirely around Michael, and only Scottie Pippen was considered an all-star-level teammate for Michael. Though he was almost always at his best, Michael was even better in the playoffs when the games were on the line. He shook off double teams—and in one case the flu—to lead his team to NBA championships. Though "His Airness" was known for his high-flying dunks, he was also named the league's best defensive player and was a constant on the All-Defensive team.

Michael won three NBA titles in a row in 1991, 1992, and 1993. After the 1993 season, he announced he was trading in his high tops for baseball cleats. Michael played for the Birmingham Barons in the minor leagues before rejoining the Bulls in the middle of the 1994–1995 season.

Michael proved to be just as dominant a player after his baseball stint as he had been before. He led the Bulls to another three-peat, winning the NBA championship in 1996, 1997, and 1998. Michael made his decision to retire a second time in 1999.

Though he will always be known as a Chicago Bulls star, Michael came out of retirement and played two additional seasons (2001–2002 and 2002–2003) for the Washington Wizards before finalizing his retirement once and for all.

MICHAEL JORDAN

Points	Rebounds	Assists
30.1	6.2	5.3

Earvin "Magic" Johnson: Los Angeles

At 6 feet 9 inches, it was hard to imagine Magic Johnson as a point guard. Yet he revolutionized the game with his no-look passes and also pulled down more than seven rebounds a game. Though his shooting skills were never given a lot of respect, he averaged 19.5 points a game during his distinguished career. In addition to his passing repertoire, Magic was a winner, leading Los Angeles to five NBA titles and setting the standard for rivalry with classic matchups with Larry Bird and the Boston Celtics.

Magic's first NBA title came in 1980, his first season. In the finals, with Kareem Abdul-Jabbar out with an injury, Magic moved to center and pulled his team together to win the championship. He could spin and pass at the same time, throw 40-foot alley-oops to his teammates for dunks, throw really fast and hard passes, and make passes behind his back as he charged toward the hoop. Magic was so deft with his passing that sometimes it wasn't only his opponents who were caught off guard; his teammates had to get used to being ready for a pass from Magic at even the most unexpected times. Magic passed Oscar Robertson's league-leading assist mark, which was later taken by Utah's John Stockton.

But Magic was the human highlight of passing, and it was just unfathomable to fans—and opponents—that a man so big could pass better than the smallest point guards. Magic was the king of the triple double—double figures in points, rebounds, and assists. He also won an Olympic gold medal with the original Dream Team in 1992. Magic could dribble with the best point guards of all time and he rebounded like a power forward. He had too many dimensions for opposing defenses to stop him.

MAGIC JOHNSON

Points	Rebounds	Assists
19.5	7.2	11.2

Point Well Taken

The point guard has to be a great ball handler with lots of speed. She has to be ready to attack and think fast. This player is in trouble. Can you see what she's up against?

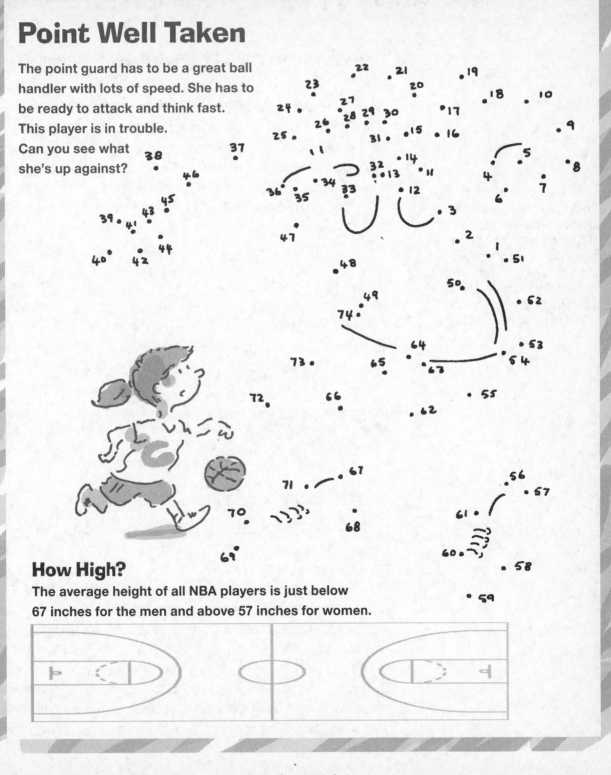

How High?

The average height of all NBA players is just below 67 inches for the men and above 57 inches for women.

Oscar Robertson: Cincinnati, Milwaukee

A 12-time All-Star, Oscar Robertson was NBA MVP in 1964 and led his team to an NBA title in 1971. Oscar, nicknamed "The Big O," was an absolute offensive machine. In the 1961–1962 season, just his second year in the league, he averaged a triple-double with 30.8 points, 12.5 rebounds, and 11.4 assists. It was a feat none of the greats who followed would ever achieve.

Oscar started out with the Cincinnati Royals in the 1960–1961 season and then became a Milwaukee Buck before the 1970–1971 season. During that time he became the top-scoring guard, and only Michael Jordan has passed him. While Oscar's point totals were eye popping, his passing skills were what left opponents scratching their heads. Oscar was 6 feet 5 inches, the first true "big" guard. So while he had lofty assist totals for even the best point guard, he had rebounding averages that would have made a power forward proud.

OSCAR ROBERTSON

Points	Rebounds	Assists
25.7	7.5	9.5

Earl Monroe: Baltimore, New York

Between 1967 and 1980, "Earl the Pearl" Monroe played the game the way Magic Johnson would play it—before there were 24-hour sports stations and nightly highlight reels on TV. Earl started his pro career when the Baltimore Bullets drafted him second overall and finished fourth in scoring his rookie year with a 24.3-points-per-game average. He earned the Rookie of the Year award in 1968, led New York to the NBA title in 1968, and was eventually inducted into the Hall of Fame. Earl was known for his circus-like moves and drew gasps from the crowd as he scored every which way imaginable. He could score off his spin moves and shot

FUN FACTS

Oscar filed a lawsuit that helped redefine the NBA draft and free agency. Oscar, who was head of the players' union, filed the suit to change the rules so that players, not just owners, got some of the ever-increasing NBA profits. It made it possible for NBA stars to make millions of dollars in salary.

in an unusual manner, yet it worked. Earl had a 46 percent success rate for field goals, which was high for a guard.

EARL MONROE

Points	Rebounds	Assists
18.8	3.0	3.9

Jerry West: Minneapolis, Los Angeles

Though he'll always be known to modern fans as the Lakers's general manager who brought in Magic Johnson, Kobe Bryant, and Shaquille O'Neal, Jerry West was a player for the ages as well; he played for both Minnesota and Los Angeles. His average of 27 points a game are matched by nearly seven assists and nearly six rebounds a game, very impressive for a guard. Jerry was the NBA finals MVP in 1969 even though the Lakers lost the title, and he helped deliver an NBA title in 1972. He was the third player in NBA history to score 25,000 points, behind Wilt Chamberlin and Oscar Robertson. Jerry also had one of the most prominent early pro buzzer beaters; at the end of regulation, his 60 footer found nothing but net to tie the Knicks in Game 3 of the 1970 NBA Finals. The humble Jerry had a unique nickname, "Zeke from Cabin Creek," the city where his rural West Virginia family picked up their mail.

JERRY WEST

Points	Rebounds	Assists
27.0	5.8	6.7

Clyde Drexler: Portland, Houston

Clyde "The Glide" Drexler, along with Michael Jordan, was part of the high-flying era of the NBA in the 1980s, at which time Clyde was one of the game's taller guards. The Hall of

Fame player averaged more than 20 points and 5.6 assists a game, yet he also pulled down more than six rebounds a game—outstanding for a guard. Though he was drafted by Portland in 1983 and twice led the Trail Blazers to runner-up finishes in the NBA finals (in 1990 and 1992), he returned to his college hometown of Houston to get his first NBA championship with the Houston Rockets in 1995. Clyde was part of the University of Houston basketball team, dubbed Phi Slamma Jamma by a local journalist. He was also a member of the original Olympic Dream Team that won gold in 1992.

CLYDE DREXLER

Points	Rebounds	Assists
20.4	6.1	5.6

Isiah Thomas: Detroit

Isiah Thomas was the consummate point guard, handing out nearly 10 assists per game yet scoring almost 20 points per game. He was seldom outplayed by his counterpart. Barely over 6 feet tall, "Zeke," as he was known, could will his team to victories with his drive and competitive nature. He guided his Detroit Pistons to back-to-back NBA championships in 1989 and 1990 and was named NBA finals MVP in 1990.

During that era, the Detroit Pistons were known as the "Bad Boys." They played a physical brand of basketball that was deplored by many of the new-school athletes but adored by blue-collar Detroit fans. Isiah played in the NBA 1981–1994 and made the All-Star team all but his last year in the league. He was only the fourth player to finish with more than 9,000 assists, joining John Stockton, Magic Johnson, and Oscar Robertson.

ISIAH THOMAS

Points	Rebounds	Assists
19.2	3.6	9.3

★ FUN FACTS ★

On the court, Isiah was a winner. Off the court, he's had far less success. Before being dismissed as the New York Knicks coach in 2008, he owned the entire Continental Basketball Association for almost two years, which ended up in bankruptcy.

Pete Maravich: Atlanta, New Orleans, Utah, Boston

"Pistol" Pete Maravich never won a title, but he was a dazzling showman of a basketball player. He played 1970–1980 and was perhaps a decade ahead of his time. His fancy passing made purists frown, but it raised his teammates' scoring averages. The 6 foot 5 inch Pete was hard for opposing players to guard because of his slight build and speed on the court. He was known for being a strong player in the regular season. Pete's teams were also known for making early playoff exits, though in fairness to Pete, his teammates struggled as well. The playoffs are regarded as more defensively oriented affairs than the free-for-all atmosphere of the regular season, a style that clearly didn't suit Pete and his teammates.

TIP-IN

Sadly, Pete died of an undiagnosed heart ailment in 1988 at age 40 after a pick-up basketball game.

PETE MARAVICH

Points	Rebounds	Assists
24.2	4.2	5.4

John Stockton: Utah

John Stockton was the prototypical "old school" point guard. At 6 feet 1 inch, he was not overly tall but was a great passer and a good floor general, which means he had a good command of running the offense and knowing where everyone was at all times. John and teammate Karl Malone led the Jazz to two NBA finals appearances but lost both. Still, John became the NBA's all-time assist leader, finishing with an amazing 15,806 assists, which averaged out to about one assist for every three minutes he played. He was also consistent, leading the Jazz to the playoffs 19 times between 1984 and 2003. John was an All-Star 10 of his years in the league. He also averaged fewer than three turnovers a game, a very low number for a point guard who was counted on to bring the ball up and run the offense up the court virtually every time. A quiet leader, John was respected as much for how he carried himself off the court as for his intensity on it. Never a trash talker or self promoter, John was a throwback to the older generations of players and was greatly respected by players and coaches for his style and character.

JOHN STOCKTON

Points	Rebounds	Assists
13.1	2.7	10.5

Bob Cousy: Boston, Cincinnati

Before Magic Johnson and Pete Maravich, Bob Cousy was a revolutionary passer of the basketball. Bob developed the no-look pass and earned the nickname "Houdini of the Hardwood" for his magical passing touch. He was also called "Mr. Basketball," "The Cooz," and the "Human Highlight Film." Bob had great teammates to get the ball to, including K.C. Jones, Tommy Heinsohn, and Bill Russell. Bob played in 13 All-Star Games in a row and won six NBA championships. He led the league in assists for eight consecutive years and even though his passing drew the most attention, he averaged more than 18 points a game for his career.

Bob almost did not end up playing basketball because he was cut twice from his high school's junior varsity team. After suffering a broken arm, he learned to shoot and pass with his left arm, which made him the consummate guard. He ended up making the high school team two years later and was on his way to greatness.

Bob had a career that spanned three decades. He played for the Boston Celtics 1950–1963. He then retired from basketball and coached at Boston College. In the 1969–1970 season, when he was 41 years old, he served as both a player and coach of the Cincinnati Royals.

★ FUN FACTS ★

Legendary Boston coach Red Auerbach did not want to draft Bob, as many coaches were wary of his razzle-dazzle style. Even though Bob was a native New Englander, Auerbach said he would not draft a "local yokel."

BOB COUSY		
Points	Rebounds	Assists
18.4	5.2	7.5

Forwards

The great forwards of the NBA were often great rebounders and great scorers, and many could dunk the basketball very effectively. Larry Bird revolutionized the position because he brought to it the ability to pass like a point guard. Today, power forwards have to be able to shut down the other team's top offensive players, but they must also be able to score themselves. They are also expected to get a lot of rebounds at both ends of the basketball court.

Larry Bird: Boston

Larry Bird did everything well. He passed, rebounded, shot, played defense—and won. Larry brought out the best in his teammates and the result was three NBA championships. He was always at his best when important games were on the line. Larry was also known for hustling so hard all the time that he would end up jumping over the scorer's table or into the stands to get a loose ball. After having great teams in the 1960s Boston had struggled in the late 1970s, but Larry changed that, becoming the face of the Celtics from 1979–1991.

With teammates such as Kevin McHale and Robert Parish, the Celtics won 10 Atlantic

Bounce Back

Rebounding is a big part of what a forward does in basketball. There are a lot of words that start with "re." Can you figure these out?

Re__ __ __
To respond to something

Re__ __ __ __ __ __ __ __
To place something again

Re__ __ __ __
To go back to where you were

Re__ __ __ __
The device you use to change channels

Re__ __ __ __ __
To lie down

Re__ __ __ __ __
To decorate and fix up again

Division titles. Larry was a 12-time All-Star team selection. He was also good at the fundamentals, leading the league four times in free-throw percentage. During one streak in his career, Larry made 71 free throws in a row. Though he was not as athletic as Michael Jordan, "Larry Legend" made seemingly impossible shots, ranging from 35-foot jumpers over defenders to layups that seemed to defy the laws of physics. He even reined in jumpers from behind the backboard on occasion.

Larry won a gold medal with the Dream Team in the 1992 Olympics, and even though he talked tough with his opponents, publicly he was understated and even humble. Through his hard work and amazing skills he became a favorite not just in Boston, but around the league. From rural French Lick, Indiana, Larry was the original Hoosier. He lived to play basketball and brought love of basketball into the lives of fans.

TIP-IN

Bobby Knight was Larry's first college coach when Larry went to play at the University of Indiana. But Larry, who was from a small town in Indiana, was overwhelmed by the big campus and dropped out of college after only a few weeks on campus. He took a year off to work and then enrolled at Indiana State University.

LARRY BIRD

Points	Rebounds	Assists
24.3	10.0	6.3

Karl Malone: Utah, Los Angeles

Karl Malone was the face of the Utah Jazz, along with John Stockton, for nearly two decades. Karl played for the Jazz 1985–2003, earning two NBA MVP awards. Though the Jazz were regulars in the playoffs, without a dominant center to complement Karl they never won an NBA title. When Karl did steer the Jazz into the NBA Finals in 1997, they were beaten by Michael Jordan's Chicago Bulls. Karl's solid fundamentals and unselfish play helped Utah establish itself as a force to be reckoned with each year in the West. Karl went to the Lakers his final year just to try to win a title, but the team came up just short, falling to the Pistons in four games in the NBA finals. Nonetheless, Karl put the "power" in power forward.

Karl was built like a bodybuilder and his opponents found it very hard to block him for rebounds. They even had difficulty stopping him as he drove the ball toward the basket. He was solid and consistent—thus his nickname, "The Mailman." He was a valuable part of the Olympic Dream Team in the 1992 Olympics.

KARL MALONE

Points	Rebounds	Assists
25.0	10.1	3.6

Julius Erving: New York, Philadelphia

He was known as "Dr. J," and before Michael Jordan came into the league, Julius Erving was the player with the high-flying dunks. He was an All-Star all 11 years he played in the league, 1977–1987, and he was clearly the most offensively dominating player of his era. Julius was the most respected player of his time and he always conducted himself as an ambassador for the league.

When he started playing professionally, Julius joined the Virginia Squires of the ABA. He was traded to the New York Nets in 1973. When the ABA and NBA merged in 1976, Julius was traded again, this time to the Philadelphia 76ers. In the five ABA seasons he played, 1971–1976, he won three scoring titles, three MVP awards, and two ABA championships. He was NBA MVP in 1981 and led Philadelphia to the NBA title in 1983. Combining both his ABA and NBA statistics, Julius remains one of the top 10 scorers in the history of the game.

At 6 feet 7 inches, Jullius was powerful yet sleek. He glided to the basket for his famous one-handed dunks that brought crowds to their feet. Dr. J's ABA dunk over 7 feet 2 inches Artis Gilmore and 6 feet 9 inches Dan Issel was the highlight of the day.

JULIUS ERVING

Points	Rebounds	Assists
22.0	6.7	3.9

John Havlicek: Boston

John Havlicek played as both a guard and a forward in his career, which spanned the years 1962–1978. He was known for his big performances in important games and helped lead the Celtics to eight championships and appeared in 13 consecutive All-Star games. John played 16 years and scored 26,395 points, grabbed 8,007 rebounds, and handed out 6,114 assists. He was one of the most balanced guard-forward players in league history. He was also a top defensive player, earning All-Defensive team honors eight times. John, the son of immigrants from Czechoslovakia, was known for tiring out his opponents by out-hustling them and constantly running from place to place on the court, earning praise from an opposing coach who said "Hondo" Havlicek was the best-conditioned player to ever play the game.

JOHN HAVLICEK

Points	Rebounds	Assists
20.8	6.3	4.8

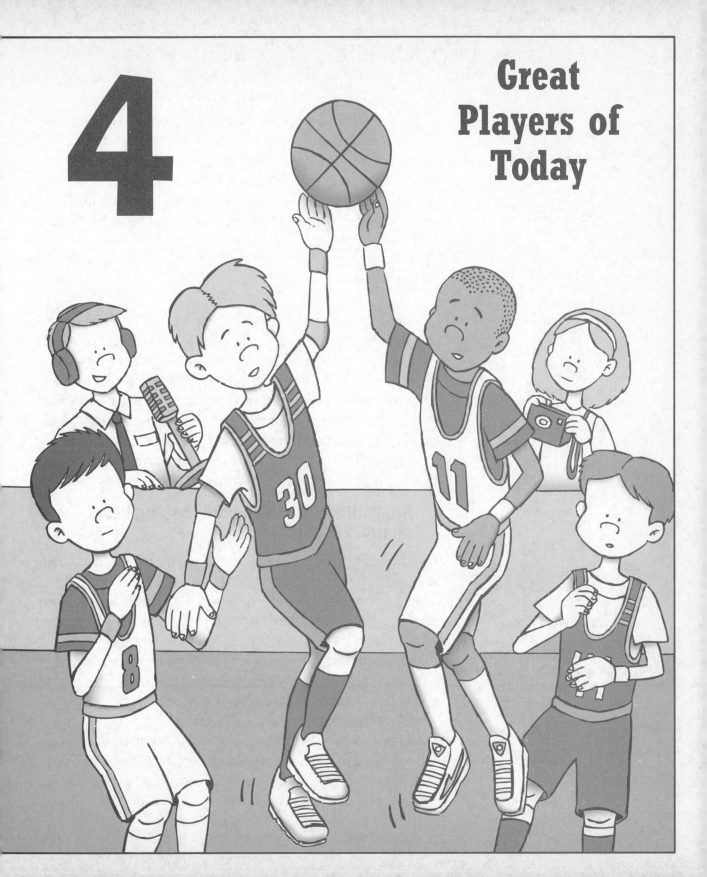

4

Great Players of Today

You have the benefit of ESPN and the Internet to give you up-to-date information on your favorite players' latest stats. Great players from today may or may not end up in the Hall of Fame, but most of these players are leaders for their teams and for the NBA. They inspire a lot of young players to take up the game and fans continue to cheer for them and wear their jerseys.

Centers

Today's great centers are different from their predecessors in one key way: They are as athletic as many of the forwards of the "old" days and are so physically strong that they can dominate with sheer muscle. These large men are very fast. In many cases, they are built more like bodybuilders than the traditional centers ever were. Gone are the tall, skinny centers who dominated the game decades ago. Today's centers can slam dunk the ball with enough force to bring down high-tech rims and backboards, yet they can also run as fast as much smaller players.

Shaquille O'Neal: Orlando, Los Angeles, Miami, Phoenix

Though he is closing in on the end of his career, Shaquille O'Neal has been a winner, leading Los Angeles to three NBA titles in a row and bringing the Miami Heat its first NBA Championship along with guard Dwyane Wade. Literally an immovable object at 7 feet 1 inch and 325 pounds, Shaquille is the quintessential big man, dunking and banking in shots after taking passes from his teammates. An occasional actor off the court, Shaq has gotten mixed reviews for his rapping skills and is among the worst free throw shooters in the game. However, his 25-points-per-game average, coupled with more than 11 rebounds a game and countless blocked shots, gives his team a chance to win every time out and forces opposing offenses to design game plans that work around his considerable stature.

FUN FACTS

Everybody loves a rhyme. Shaq's dominant style of basketball came to be known as a "Shaq attack." When teams start fouling Shaq to get him to the free throw line, you might hear the term "hack-a-Shaq."

SHAQUILLE O'NEAL

Points	Rebounds	Assists
25.2	11.5	2.7

Tim Duncan: San Antonio

An all-around player and a great teammate, Tim Duncan has been among the most prolific big men in the modern-day NBA, winning titles both with David Robinson and without him. Tim has been the league MVP and the NBA finals MVP. He is considered somewhat "old school" because he is very humble. For his jump shots he often banks the ball off the backboard, which is harder for defenders to stop and is regarded as a more reliable way to make a basket. Tim is just an inch under 7 feet tall, but he can run the floor with most forwards. He is also a very good defensive player. An excellent rebounder and scorer, Tim has been on the NBA's All-Defensive Team every season.

Matching Sets

A lot of players help with charities because they want to give back to their community. Sometimes people give so much that it can get confusing. Can you tell which sports equipment goes with which player?

TIP-IN

Tim's sister Tricia competed for the U.S. Virgin Islands in swimming at the 1988 Summer Olympics. He might have ended up becoming an Olympic swimmer himself if his community's pool had not been destroyed during Hurricane Hugo in 1989.

Off the court, Tim founded the Tim Duncan Foundation, which raises money for educational opportunities, youth sports, and health research. The foundation sometimes gives free tickets to students who show they work hard and have high character. Tim started the organization to give back to the communities that mean the most to him—the U.S. Virgin Islands, where he grew up; North Carolina, where he went to college; and Texas, where he currently lives.

TIM DUNCAN

Points	Rebounds	Assists
21.6	11.8	3.1

Yao Ming: Houston

Yao Ming is an international player who is bringing the NBA to entirely new audiences around the world. At 7 feet 6 inches, he is one of the tallest players in league history. With his kind demeanor and soft-spoken style—in his culture it is considered disrespectful to show other players up or to brag about yourself off the court—Yao is a fan favorite, and many in China stay up through the night to watch him play for the Houston Rockets.

YAO MING

Points	Rebounds	Assists
19.0	9.2	1.6

Guards

Today's great NBA guards are stronger and faster than they have ever been. Whereas decades ago guards were mostly outside shooters, the guards of today are taller, but they're just as fast and as agile as their smaller predecessors. Some guards even rebound just as well as many forwards. The guards of today are expected to be a big part of the offense. They must score from anywhere in the offensive end, whether it is driving to the basket for a dunk or shooting a three pointer.

Kobe Bryant: Los Angeles

Seldom has a player coming out of high school had such an impact as a guard. A lot of fans don't remember that the Lakers did not draft Kobe Bryant; rather, he was drafted by Charlotte before Lakers general manager Jerry West quickly traded to get him. At just under 18.5 years old, Kobe was the youngest player to start an NBA game.

Kobe has an excellent outside shot, and at 6 feet 6 inches he can drive inside for layups and dunks. Though his 30-plus point average draws a lot of attention, he has also been named to the NBA's All-Defensive Team. He teamed with Shaquille O'Neal to lead the Lakers to three consecutive NBA Championships. In 2008, without Shaquille, Kobe was named NBA MVP and led his team to the NBA finals, where the Lakers lost to the Boston Celtics.

FUN FACTS

Kobe Bryant entered the NBA straight out of high school and has played for the Los Angeles Lakers since the 1996–1997 season. He won three consecutive championships with the Lakers between 2000 and 2002. He is an excellent shooter, scoring 81 points in a game against the Toronto Raptors in 2006.

KOBE BRYANT

Points	Rebounds	Assists
25.0	5.3	4.6

Chris Paul: New Orleans

Chris Paul went from nowhere to the center of the NBA universe in a hurry, emerging as one of the top guards in the league. Though his career scoring average is a relatively modest 18 points a game, he averaged more than 21 in the 2007–2008 season, a year in which he led his New Orleans

Hornets deep into the playoffs and averaged 24.1 points and 11.3 rebounds per game.

The fleet-of-foot 6 footer can distribute the ball like a traditional point guard, but can also drive to the basket with his quick moves. Chris is known for his good court vision and basketball sense.

Family is important to Chris, and when his grandfather passed away unexpectedly during his senior year of high school, he scored 61 points on the day of his grandfather's funeral—one point for every year of his grandpa's life. If you don't see Chris on the basketball court, look for him in the bowling alley, where he is an elite-level amateur bowler.

CHRIS PAUL

Points	Rebounds	Assists
18.2	4.5	9.5

Jason Kidd: Phoenix, New Jersey, Dallas

In the post Magic Johnson era, Jason Kidd is widely regarded as the best pure point guard in the league. At 6 feet 4 inches, Jason is tall by traditional point guard standards but passes with the best of them. He has averaged almost seven assists per game throughout his long career; during three seasons he averaged more than 10 assists per game. Jason has also been named to the NBA's All-Defensive Team, so he does not take a break or slack off when his team doesn't have the ball. In 2007–2008, Jason averaged nearly seven rebounds a game— almost unheard of for a point guard in the modern era.

JASON KIDD

Points	Rebounds	Assists
14.2	6.7	9.3

Gilbert Arenas: Washington

One of many University of Arizona players to have a significant impact on the NBA, Gilbert Arenas has also emerged as the face of Washington's franchise. His nearly 23-points-per-game career average demonstrates what a consistent scorer the 6 foot 4 inch guard is. Gilbert is one of the league's most explosive offensive players and averages 5.5 assists per game as well. He is also very active in several charitable causes.

GILBERT ARENAS

Points	Rebounds	Assists
22.8	4.2	5.5

TIP-IN

Gilbert has one of the more unique nicknames. He is called "Hibachi," which is a smallish Japanese grill that heats up in a hurry—just like Gilbert when he starts scoring many baskets in a row.

Allen Iverson: Philadelphia, Denver, Detroit

The explosive, enigmatic offensive juggernaut has everything but an NBA title on his professional resume. Allen Iverson, nicknamed "The Answer," has provided the ultimate question mark to NBA defenders. His deadly crossover move often freezes opponents in their shoes as he drives to the basket. A talented shooter, Allen has averaged more than 30 points a game five different times. He draws so many defenders that he is able to average more than six assists per game. Allen was a cocaptain and leading scorer for the 2004 U.S. Olympic Team.

ALLEN IVERSON

Points	Rebounds	Assists
27.7	3.8	6.3

Dwyane Wade, Miami

The Miami Heat were looking for prominence in the NBA, and pairing high-flying scoring guard Dwyane Wade and Shaquille O'Neal put them well on their way to winning their first NBA championship. Dwayne earned the NBA finals MVP

★ FUN FACTS ★

The Detroit Pistons play in a building called the Palace of Auburn Hills and Allen became one of the "palace guards" when he joined the Pistons in 2008. The arena's name also works well for Allen's teammate, Tayshaun Prince, who is sometimes called "the Prince of the Palace."

award in 2006, the same year *Sports Illustrated* named him Sportsman of the Year.

DWYANE WADE

Points	Rebounds	Assists
23.9	4.8	6.5

Forwards

The power forwards of today are the most athletic the game has ever seen. In the past, a 7 footer like the Celtics' Kevin Garnett would always have been a center because he usually would have been the tallest player on the court. But with so many players 7 feet or taller, height is no longer something altogether unique in the NBA. Power forwards can be fast and powerful, like Karl Malone was, but they can also be tall, lean, and fast, like Kevin Garnett. These players are often better shooters from the outside than their predecessors from decades ago, but they are still counted on to do a lot of rebounding at both ends of the court.

Kevin Garnett: Minnesota, Boston

When the Boston Celtics acquired the nearly 7 foot Kevin Garnett before the start of the 2007–2008 season, they had one thing in mind: an NBA championship. Kevin, who was drafted out of high school by the Minnesota Timberwolves, delivered a championship to the Celtics his first season with them. Though he plays near the basket as power forward, there might not be a sleeker, leaner big man in the NBA who can run the court as well as Kevin. He made the All-Defensive Team five years in a row and was named NBA MVP in 2004 and Defensive Player of the Year in 2008. Kevin is also a very good shot blocker; while playing for the Timberwolves he set the team record with 163 blocks in one season.

KEVIN GARNETT

Points	Rebounds	Assists
20.4	11.2	4.4

Paul Pierce: Boston

Paul Pierce came into his own as a superstar in the 2007–2008 season and helped the "Big Three"—himself, Kevin Garnett, and Ray Allen—lead Boston to the 2008 NBA Championship, in which Paul was named the finals MVP. Paul is a scoring machine, but he posts solid numbers both rebounding and passing the ball as well. In the 2008 NBA Playoffs, with Kevin and Ray struggling offensively, Paul took the team on his shoulders and carried them past the Los Angeles Lakers.

PAUL PIERCE

Points	Rebounds	Assists
23.1	6.4	3.9

LeBron James, Cleveland

Few players have come into the league with as much hype and pressure as LeBron "King" James, who was drafted first overall to rescue the Cleveland Cavaliers from years of mediocrity. LeBron has taken the team to the NBA finals, but has yet to win the crown that would fit his nickname so well. However, he is one of the most dominant players in the game. At 6 feet 8 inches and 250 pounds, LeBron can dribble and pass like a guard but can also drive to the basket against taller defenders to dunk, score a layup, or draw a foul. By drawing so many defenders to himself, LeBron has been able to dish out almost as many assists per game as rebounds. Though he has played with few All-Star teammates in his career, he has made Cleveland a regular in the playoffs. LeBron was named NBA MVP in 2009.

LEBRON JAMES

Points	Rebounds	Assists
27.3	6.9	6.6

Tracy McGrady: Toronto, Orlando, Houston

After being drafted by Toronto right out of high school, Tracy McGrady took a few years to get his NBA feet underneath him. Traded to Orlando, Tracy became a perennial All-Star and in the 2007–2008 season he led the Houston Rockets to one of the longest winning streaks in league history—22 games. At 6 feet 8 inches and 203 pounds, Tracy is taller than the guards who try to defend him and quicker than the forwards who are assigned to him. He has been named a favorite player in polls by *Sports Illustrated Kids* and was dubbed a "Good Guy in Sports" by the *Sporting News*.

TRACY MCGRADY

Points	Rebounds	Assists
22.4	6.2	4.7

Chris Bosh: Toronto

Chris Bosh, who can play forward or center, averaged 22-plus points and more than nine rebounds a game from 2006–2008 and emerged as a legitimate MVP candidate. At 6 feet 10 inches, Chris has been the focal point of the Raptors's resurgence in the East.

CHRIS BOSH

Points	Rebounds	Assists
18.9	9.0	2.1

Opposites Attract

One of the first great players of basketball—in fact, he was called Mr. Basketball—was George Mikan. His training regimen included shadow boxing, rope-skipping, and ballet! Sometimes things fit together perfectly even when they don't look like they should. Can you match these words with their opposite?

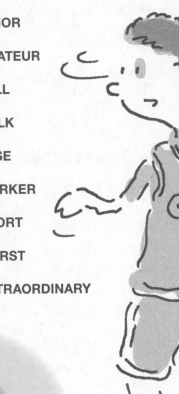

AVERAGE	MINOR
PLAYER	AMATEUR
PROFESSIONAL	PULL
PUSH	WALK
BEST	LOSE
WIN	WORKER
TALL	SHORT
MAJOR	WORST
RUN	EXTRAORDINARY

Major Milestone

In 1950, Earl Lloyd became a member of the Washington Capitols. He was the first African American to play in the NBA.

Score!

This scorekeeper is having trouble with numbers and letters. Can you help him unscramble the strings of letters here? Only one of them has all the letters to spell BASKETBALL SCORE.

OBASTALBLCSKRE

TKELSBCERALBOS

OCASSTABLLEEBKE

RALOKESCCASTBLE

KCLEOASBABSLRET

ALTLSBRSSEOAECK

KBSABCSLELEROAT

Carmelo Anthony: Denver

With a career scoring average above 24 points a game, Carmelo Anthony has made the Denver Nuggets a regular playoff participant in the West. In his one and only season at Syracuse, Carmelo led the Orangemen to an NCAA championship. He was also a member of the 2004 Olympic Dream Team in Athens and the 2008 Redeem Team in Beijing.

CARMELO ANTHONY

Points	Rebounds	Assists
24.4	6.0	3.0

Dirk Nowitzki: Dallas

Dirk Nowitzki, the 7-foot center from Germany, has become the face of the Dallas Mavericks's franchise during his time in the NBA. Dirk is also known to stop eating his dinner and let his food get cold just to sign autographs for kids who approach him. What has made Dirk such a unique big man is that he can shoot the ball so well from the outside. In his career, he has made almost 40 percent of the three-point shots he has taken. He was named NBA MVP in 2007. Regarded by general managers as the best international player in the league, the one thing that has eluded Dirk is an NBA title, though the Mavericks regularly make deep runs in the playoffs.

DIRK NOWITZKI

Points	Rebounds	Assists
22.4	8.6	2.7

5 Women's Basketball

College Women's Basketball

In 1892, the year after Dr. James Naismith invented what we know to be basketball, the first game of women's basketball was played. Women's college basketball began in 1893 with teams starting at Iowa State College, Carleton, Mount Holyoke, and Tulane.

In 1896, Stanford played the University of California at Berkeley in the first women's intercollegiate game, with Stanford winning, 2-1. Rather than the eventual 5-on-5 format familiar to current fans, that game was played 9-on-9. The women's game has come a long way since then.

Title IX and the 1970s

The 1970s were a critical period of growth for women's college basketball. The sport had languished in the shadows of prominent men's programs because the men tended to get more funding. In the 1970s, the International Olympic Committee added women's basketball as a medal sport, and it debuted to immense popularity at the 1976 Olympic Games.

The landscape changed for college women's sports, including basketball, when Congress passed Title IX in 1972. Title IX was designed to make sure that women's sports received just as much funding as men's sports. If a school offers a sport for men, it must also offer one for women. It also evened out scholarships for men's and women's teams, which was important for women's basketball programs. According to NCAA figures, participation in women's sports increased by roughly 400 percent in the 30-plus years since Title IX was enacted.

★ **FUN FACTS** ★

In 2000, University of Tennessee standout Michelle Snow became the third-ever woman to dunk in a college game. In 2009, Pat Summitt picked up her 1,000th career win as a college women's coach, becoming the coach with the most wins in all of basketball—college and professional.

Women's NCAA Basketball Today

The NCAA began its women's NCAA basketball tournament in 1982, and Louisiana Tech beat Cheyney State in the final game. There were 32 teams in the field the first four years, 40 teams from 1986 to 1988, and 48 teams from 1989 to 1993. In 1994, it expanded to 64 teams, just like the men's tournament. And like the men's tournament, those teams are chosen through a mixture of conference champions and teams that receive invitations.

Tennessee, led by Hall of Fame coach Pat Summitt, and the University of Connecticut became powerhouses in the sport. Tennessee won three titles in a row from 1996–98. Connecticut won four of five NCAA Championships from 2000–2004. Tennessee won back-to-back titles in 2007 and 2008, and Connecticut claimed the 2009 NCAA championship.

The women's NCAA tournament still has fewer viewers than men, but it has drawn impressive attendance and has TV contracts that support it financially and promote the sport in millions of homes each year. The creation of the WNBA also boosted the college women's game.

The WNBA

The Women's National Basketball Association was formed in 1996 by the NBA. The first WNBA games were played in June 1997. The Houston Comets quickly emerged as a dominant team in the new league. Sheryl Swoopes and Cynthia Cooper—the WNBA's first Most Valuable Player—with the Comets won the first WNBA title. Lisa Leslie of the Los Angeles Sparks became the first player to capture all three MVP awards in the same season (regular season, all-star, and championship MVP honors).

FUN FACTS

While the NBA has 12-minute quarters, the WNBA has 10-minute quarters. The women's basketball is 28.5 inches around—an inch smaller in diameter than the basketball used by the men. After starting with a 30-second shot clock, the WNBA switched to a 24-second shot clock, which is the same as the NBA.

TIP-IN

Women's basketball did not become an Olympic sport until the 1976 Games in Montreal. The United States women lost in the gold medal game to the Soviet Union, leaving America with a silver medal. The bronze went to Bulgaria.

Three's a Charm

On March 21, 1893, the first women's collegiate game was played at Smith College in Northampton, Massachusetts. The physical education teacher, Senda Berenson, must have liked the number 3. There were 3 zones with 3 players allowed in each zone. Each player could hold the ball for 3 seconds and dribble 3 times before passing.

If the ball was passed 5 times in one play, what is the maximum number of times it could be dribbled?

LADIES ONLY!

In 1893, it was considered inappropriate for men to watch women playing a sport such as basketball, so all the doors to the gym were locked for the first game at Smith College.

Women's leagues had failed in the past, in part because they could not get deals with major television networks to bring in money. But the WNBA had contracts with NBC, ESPN, and Lifetime Television. The WNBA season starts after the NBA season and runs through the summer, so basketball fans can watch their favorite game all year long.

Eight teams were part of the WNBA's first season. The Eastern Conference had the Charlotte Sting, Cleveland Rockers, Houston Comets, and New York Liberty. The Western Conference had the Los Angeles Sparks, Phoenix Mercury, Sacramento Monarchs, and Utah Starzz.

Teams no longer play in Charlotte, Cleveland, Houston, or Utah, but the league has expanded to thirteen teams. The Eastern Conference includes the Detroit Shock, Connecticut Sun, Indiana Fever, New York Liberty, Washington Mystics, Chicago Sky, and Atlanta Dream; the Western Conference includes the San Antonio Silver Stars, Seattle Storm, Los Angeles Sparks, Minnesota Lynx, Sacramento Monarchs, and Phoenix Mercury.

Great Players

Though the women's league does not get as much media attendance or media coverage as the men's league, the players practice just as hard and the fundamentals in the women's leagues, both in college and professional, can be superior to the men's game. You don't hear as much about individual players in the women's league—the team concept is so strong that it cannot be undervalued. Nevertheless, here are some of the great women's players from yesterday and today.

Nancy Lieberman

Nancy Lieberman brought the no-look pass to the women's game, and before Magic Johnson ever suited up for the L.A.

Lakers, she was known as "Lady Magic." She played collegiate basketball at Old Dominion and led her school to a pair of national championships. Nancy also played two years in the United States Basketball League and played for the Washington Generals, which was the touring opponent for the Harlem Globetrotters. She was also the youngest member of the U.S. Women's Olympic team that won a silver medal at the 1976 Olympics. In 1997, though almost 40 years old, Nancy played one season for the WNBA's inaugural campaign for the Phoenix Mercury.

Cheryl Miller

Cheryl Miller was a dominant, free-wheeling player for the University of Southern California. She led the team to NCAA titles in 1983 and 1984. She was a leader of the team that won Olympic gold in 1984. A Naismith Hall of Famer, Cheryl was widely regarded as the best women's basketball player of all time when she retired. At USC, she set records for points—3,018—and rebounds—1,534. After working as an NBA commentator, Cheryl joined the WNBA as a general manager and coach. She now works as a basketball reporter.

Teresa Edwards

Though she came along before the WNBA's glory days, few have accomplished more in women's basketball than Teresa Edwards, who made her name playing professionally overseas. She also has the unprecedented distinction of being the only five-time female U.S. Olympic basketball player. The point guard led the University of Georgia to a pair of Final Four appearances before leading Team USA to four gold medals and one bronze Olympic medal. Teresa played for the fledgling American Basketball League before it folded and was the only ABL player to score more than 40 points in a game. The ABL was a women's professional league that was started in 1996 but folded in 1998 because it didn't have enough money.

★ FUN FACTS ★

Cheryl's family had a lot of athletic talent. Her brother Reggie was one of the NBA's great shooters during his career with the Indiana Pacers and another brother, Darrell, was a Major League Baseball catcher for four years with the California Angels.

Rebecca Lobo

One of the best college basketball players of all time, Rebecca Lobo helped Connecticut become a force in women's college basketball. There was no stopping Rebecca; at 6 feet 4 inches, she was very agile and graceful with the ball and was seldom beaten for a rebound. She set her state's high school scoring record with 2,710 points in Massachusetts and at UConn she became the nation's best player in 1995, leading the Huskies to the National Championship and a perfect 35-0 season. That year, Rebecca won Naismith and College Player of the Year awards. Her WNBA career with the New York Liberty started out strong, but a torn knee ligament brought her pro career to a premature end.

Ann Meyers

Ann Meyers was the first woman to sign a contract with an NBA team, getting a three-day tryout with the Indiana Pacers. Though she was cut from the team, the following year Ann

Pick Up the Pieces

These girls are looking for a game of pick up, but something has gone wrong. Can you put this back together and see what it is?

was drafted into the Women's Professional Basketball League and played just one season, 1979–1980, in which she was named Most Valuable Player. But her standout performances were as an amateur. As a high school senior in 1974, Ann became the first prep player named to a U.S. Basketball Team. She followed that up with a spot on the 1976 U.S. Olympic team, which won silver. She was also UCLA's first female full-ride scholarship student athlete. As a Lady Bruin, the 5 foot 9 inch Ann had a quadruple-double—20 points, 14 rebounds, 10 assists, and 10 steals—the only player, male or female, to do that in school history. Ann led UCLA to the 1978 National Championship.

WNBA Stars

The WNBA was founded in 1996 and started play in 1997, building off the momentum of the 1996 Olympics in which the U.S. women's team won the gold medal and gained a lot of attention in the media. Most teams are in cities that also have NBA teams. The exception was the Connecticut Sun, which is located in a state that also has one of the nation's most successful and high profile college women's programs, the University of Connecticut. The only other team not to have an NBA team in the same city is the Seattle Storm, though that only came about when the Seattle Super-Sonics relocated to Oklahoma City.

Cynthia Cooper: Houston Comets

Cynthia Cooper is one of the mainstays of the WNBA; she won four WNBA Championships as a guard with the Houston Comets. As a player, Cynthia was a scoring machine, with a career average of 21 points per game. She is the league's all-time points-per-game leader. Cynthia had a 92-game streak in which she scored double figures while in the WNBA. She was inducted into the Women's Basketball Hall of Fame in 2009.

CYNTHIA COOPER

Points	Rebounds	Assists
21.0	4.9	3.2

Sheryl Swoopes: Houston Comets, Seattle Storm

Sheryl Swoopes is the first WNBA player to earn league MVP honors three times. Though her 16-points-per-game career scoring average is eye popping, she's also been the league's most valuable player of the year in 2000, 2002, and 2005 and its defensive player of the year in 2000, 2002, and 2003. Sheryl also led the Houston Comets to four WNBA championships, including one in the league's first season. She also has three Olympic gold medals.

SHERYL SWOOPES

Points	Rebounds	Assists
16.2	5.1	3.4

Diana Taurasi: Phoenix Mercury

A career 20-points-per-game scorer in the WNBA, Diana Taurasi showed how complete she is as a player by averaging more than four assists and four rebounds per game as well. As a college player, Diana was the ultimate winner, leading her team to National Championships three years in a row—2002, 2003, and 2004. She finished college as the first Big East player with more than 2,000 points, 600 rebounds, and 600 assists.

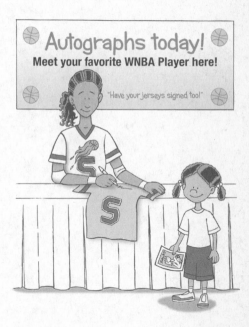

Autographs today!
Meet your favorite WNBA Player here!
"Have your jerseys signed too!"

DIANA TAURASI

Points	Rebounds	Assists
20.0	4.2	4.1

Candace Parker, Los Angeles Sparks

In the 2008 season—her rookie year—Candace Parker averaged 19 points a game, almost 10 rebounds, and exactly four assists for the Los Angeles Sparks. She was named the female athlete of the year by the Associated Press that year. Candace was the college player of the year in 2007, when she led Tennessee to a National Championship. Though Tennessee has had great college players through the decades, Candace was the fastest one to score 1,000 points, doing that in just her 56th career game. She accomplished all that in just two years at Tennessee, despite having to redshirt as a freshman because of a pair of knee injuries.

CANDACE PARKER

Points	Rebounds	Assists
18.9	9.4	3.7

Lisa Leslie, Los Angeles Sparks

Lisa Leslie, who once scored 101 points in the first half of a high school game, won the WNBA MVP award three times. She is a well-balanced force in the front court and back, averaging 17.4 points and 9.4 rebounds per game. Lisa has won two WNBA titles and is the league's all-time leading scorer.

LISA LESLIE

Points	Rebounds	Assists
17.4	9.4	2.3

Amazing Athletes

Sometimes you have to have a good eye to spot a good player on the court. Can you find the players on this court?

Sue Bird • Tamika Catchings • Lisa Leslie • Nancy Lieberman • Cheryl Miller • Sheryl Swoopes • Rebecca Lobo

```
H C H E R Y L M I L L E R E R
K V K E L D I I U N B O P S U
D U I J K X S U E B I R D T E
N V E I D H A L F L D F E Y E
A N A N C Y L I E B E R M A N
O O J S W C E H T A M I L L E
S H E R Y L S W O O P E S M I
C H E C A T L C W O B I R B S
N A N C E L I B O O R N A M L
R E B R E B E C C A L O B O R
T A M I K A C A T C H I N G S
```

I GOT YOU, BABE

One of basketball's first famous players was Babe Didrikson. She played in the 1920s. The Associated Press named her the greatest female athlete of the first half of the twentieth century. In addition to basketball, she excelled in other sports, including golf, swimming, and track and field.

Tally Ho!

Home 72 Guest 79

The final score of this game was 72–79. Which groups of numbers add up to those scores?

20 + 40 + 10 + 3 = _____

25 + 25 + 15 + 6 = _____

34 + 10 + 8 + 10 + 10 = _____

11 + 11 + 11 + 11 + 25 = _____

1 + 1 + 60 + 3 + 13 = _____

22 + 22 + 22 + 10 = _____

9 + 9 + 9 + 27 + 26 = _____

16 + 10 + 10 + 10 + 10 + 23 = _____

The WNBA's All-Decade Team

In 2006, the WNBA selected its All-Decade team after the league's 10th year:

WNBA ALL-DECADE TEAM

Name	WNBA Team (Current/Last Team)
Sue Bird	Seattle Storm
Tamika Catchings	Indiana Fever
Cynthia Cooper	Houston Comets
Yolanda Griffith	Sacramento Monarchs
Lauren Jackson	Seattle Storm
Lisa Leslie	Los Angeles Sparks
Katie Smith	Detroit Shock/Minnesota Lynx
Dawn Staley	Houston Comets/Charlotte Sting
Sheryl Swoopes	Houston Comets
Tina Thompson	Houston Comets

HONORABLE MENTION

Name	WNBA Team (Current/Last Team)
Ruthie Bolton	Sacramento Monarchs
Chamique Holdsclaw	Los Angeles Sparks/Washington Mystics
Ticha Penicheiro	Sacramento Monarchs
Diana Taurasi	Phoenix Mercury
Teresa Weatherspoon	Los Angeles Sparks/New York Liberty

6

Coaches

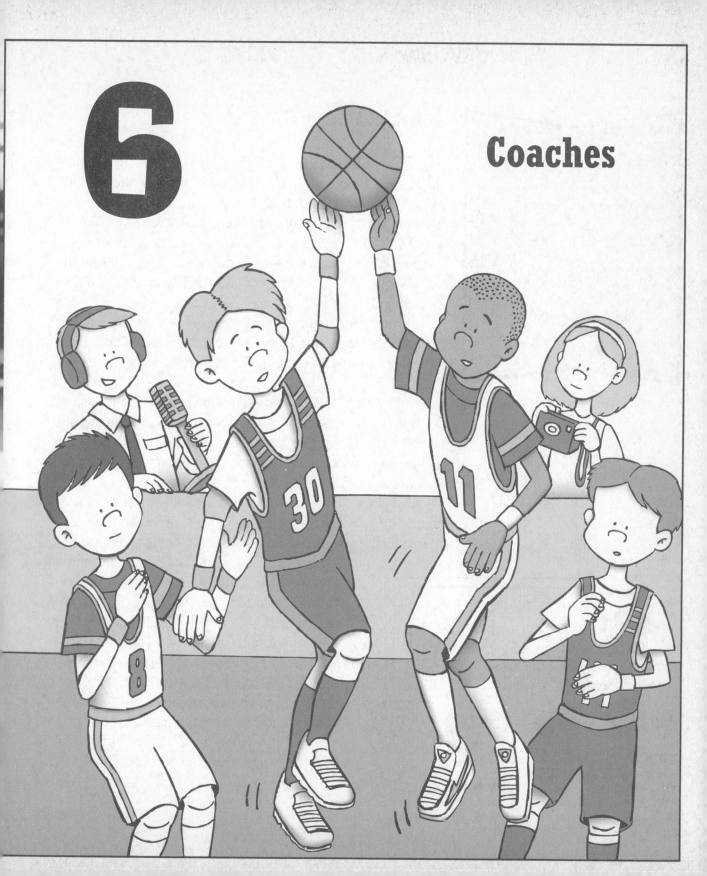

John Wooden

John Wooden was a coach through and through. Keeping college basketball in the nation's mindset while the NBA gained popularity, John built the most consistent, successful program in the history of college basketball. At UCLA, he won a record 10 national championships and groomed such future NBA greats as Kareem Abdul-Jabbar and Bill Walton. Dubbed the "Wizard of Westwood," the city in which UCLA is located, John was always a dignified man.

John's career college coaching record was 885-203, winning a little more than 80 percent of his games. He coached 27 seasons at UCLA, stepping down in 1975. He won seven national championships in a row—1966–1973—and amassed a record of 38 NCAA tournament wins in a row. John also set the regular-season wins-in-a-row record with 88. He is also the only coach to guide four undefeated teams (all four went 31-0), and he was the first person to be inducted into the Hall of Fame as both a player and coach.

As a player, John captained Purdue for two successful years as a guard, winning a pair of Big 10 titles and the 1932 national championship. Before beginning his college coaching career, John taught English at South Bend Central High School, near the Notre Dame campus, and coached the high school to a record of 218-42. His incredible journey then took him into the military, as an officer in the Navy for three years during World War II. After the war, he served as athletic director, coach, and teacher at Indiana Teachers College, later renamed Indiana State University—the college where Larry Bird would eventually star.

Follow the Rules!

If you want your team to win, it helps to have a great coach. This coach is very tough. Can you see how these players can get through the obstacle course?

☆ 87 ☆

Arnold "Red" Auerbach

When Arnold "Red" Auerbach died in late 2006 at age 89, the NBA lost a legend, but he left a lot of memories behind. Red actually started with the Washington Capitols and the Tri-Cities Hawks before joining Boston, where he would be part of the franchise for the next 57 years. He got off to the right start in Boston, trading two players to St. Louis for the right to draft Bill Russell, the cornerstone Red built an NBA dynasty around. He coached the Celtics to nine championships, including eight in a row. Even though he could have added more titles to his coaching resume, Red stepped back into the general manager role, acquiring key players to engineer an additional pair of titles in 1968 and 1969.

The Celtics struggled in the 1970s, but when Red saw Larry Bird, he saw the future of his franchise. Getting Bird in the coop was solid, but Red knew he needed to get several more players to complement Bird's skill. He drew the 1st and 13th picks of the 1981 draft to get center Robert Parish and a draft pick, which he used to draft Kevin McHale. He rescued Dennis Johnson and Bill Walton from their careers in the Northwest and revived them, fitting them into the mix to make the Celtics a smart, deep team. The addition of heady guard Danny Ainge, who annoyed opponents to the point of fits, was sheer brilliance.

Pat Summitt

When someone says "the best coach in history," there is usually room for debate. When it comes to women's basketball, there is no debate, because no one has ever equaled the success of Pat Summitt. And the University of Tennessee Hall of Fame coach just keeps putting winners on the court year after year. After repeating an NCAA championship in 2008—for her eighth NCAA title at Tennessee—Pat remains the coach with

WORDS TO KNOW

DNP-Coach's Decision
DNP shows up in box scores, and it means "Did Not Play." Coach's Decision means the coach chose not to put the player in the game. The player did not miss the game because of injury, suspension, or any other reason.

Final Four
The Final Four for the college women and men are simply the four teams left in the semifinals and finals of the NCAA tournament. The teams are the champions from the four brackets of the NCAA tournament.

Everybody Chant

Words have a lot of power to motivate us. This player has decided to write a song for her team. It looks like she's having trouble with the final word in each line. Can you help her out? (Hint: the last words all rhyme.)

The game is on, it's getting l___ ___ ___

The score's close, 87 to 8 ___

It's up to you to decide their f___ ___ ___!

Make us proud of our s ___ ___ ___ ___;

Let's tell the players we think they're g ___ ___ ___ ___!

A coach was having trouble with one of his players, so he took him aside for a talk. "What's the problem? Is it ignorance or apathy?" The player replied, "I don't know and I don't care!"

the most wins in college history, women's or men's. Through 2009, she had won 1,007 games while losing just 193—a winning percentage of 80 percent. Under Pat, Tennessee made a record 16 consecutive Final Fours in a row and a record 27 appearances in the Sweet 16. She has produced 12 Olympic players, and every single one of her players who completed their eligibility at Tennessee graduated with their degrees.

Pat "Riles" Riley

With his slicked back hair, Pat Riley was the conductor of the Lakers's "Showtime" production that included Magic Johnson, James Worthy, Kareem Abdul-Jabbar, and three NBA titles. Pat left to coach the New York Knicks, where he showed he could coach a physical style of play. Despite taking New York to the finals, he could not win an NBA Championship. Coaxed to Florida to get the expansion Miami Heat up to the elite NBA standards, Pat built a solid group of veterans around young superstar Dwyane Wade. Once Pat was able to land Shaquille O'Neal from the Lakers, the Heat turned up the temperature on the rest of the league and brought Miami its first NBA Championship.

Mike "Coach K" Krzyzewski

Considering where his playing and coaching roots were planted, it's no surprise that Mike Krzyzewski's teams are disciplined and fundamentally sound. Mike played and coached at the Military Academy at West Point. He left the Army for Duke in 1980, and thus began a dominating coaching performance for the ages. Under Mike, Duke has won three national championships, and he has more than 800 coaching wins. He has been National Coach of the Year 12 times.

Dean Smith

When he retired, North Carolina's Dean Smith had the most wins in college basketball history. But for the Tar Heels, Dean was more than a coach—he was an institution. Dean first coached three years as an assistant coach at North Carolina before taking the head job. In 36 years as head coach, he won 879 games and had just 254 losses. Dean's Tar Heels won National Championships in 1982 and 1993, and 96 percent of his student athletes graduated. Dean also coached the U.S. Olympic team to the gold medal in 1976.

Bobby Knight

Bobby Knight won a pair of national championships at the University of Indiana and leads all men's college basketball coaches with 902 career victories. His teams, with a few exceptions, did not have superstars who turned into NBA greats, but they played good defense and had solid fundamentals—and they never stopped hustling. Bobby also coached the U.S. Olympic Basketball team to a gold medal in 1984. After coaching at Indiana, he moved on to coach in the Big 12 at Texas Tech University before stepping aside. Bobby was succeeded at Tech by his son, longtime assistant coach Pat Knight.

Crazy Coach

Coaches often use code so the other team can't understand their next play. But this coach looks like he's just being silly. Can you figure out the first letter of these silly sayings?

___un ___ound
___obin ___egularly

___on't ___ribble ___owntown

___erfect ___layers ___lay ___olitely

___onight ___all ___eams
___ake ___urns

___rateful ___uards
___et ___oals

Don Haskins

Don Haskins set the bar high, winning 719 games as a head coach, including the National Championship with Texas Western in 1966. At the time Don coached, not all coaches were giving black players a chance to play. Don was the first Division I coach to start five black players, and his team beat a heavily favored University of Kentucky team for the national championship. In his 38-year career, Don took his team to 14 NCAA tournaments.

Adolph Rupp

Adolph Rupp's success in winning games and championships for the University of Kentucky are part of college basketball's history. His Wildcats claimed four national Championships in the 1940s and 1950s. Adolph built a program at Kentucky that to this day is seen as one of the premier programs in the country and has drawn talented coaches such as Rick Pitino to Lexington. Adolph was a back-up player for legendary Kansas coach Phog Allen, who was assisted by the very founder of basketball, James Naismith.

Phil Jackson

As coach of the Chicago Bulls, Phil Jackson had the best player in the world in Michael Jordan. But outside of their core players—Michael and Scottie Pippen—the Bulls had to rely on role players. Phil's six titles with the Chicago Bulls were a run not seen in decades. He added three more championship wins with Kobe Bryant, Shaquille O'Neal, and the Lakers. In 2009, he won his tenth NBA championship with Kobe and the Lakers, passing coaching great Red Auerbach for most titles ever.

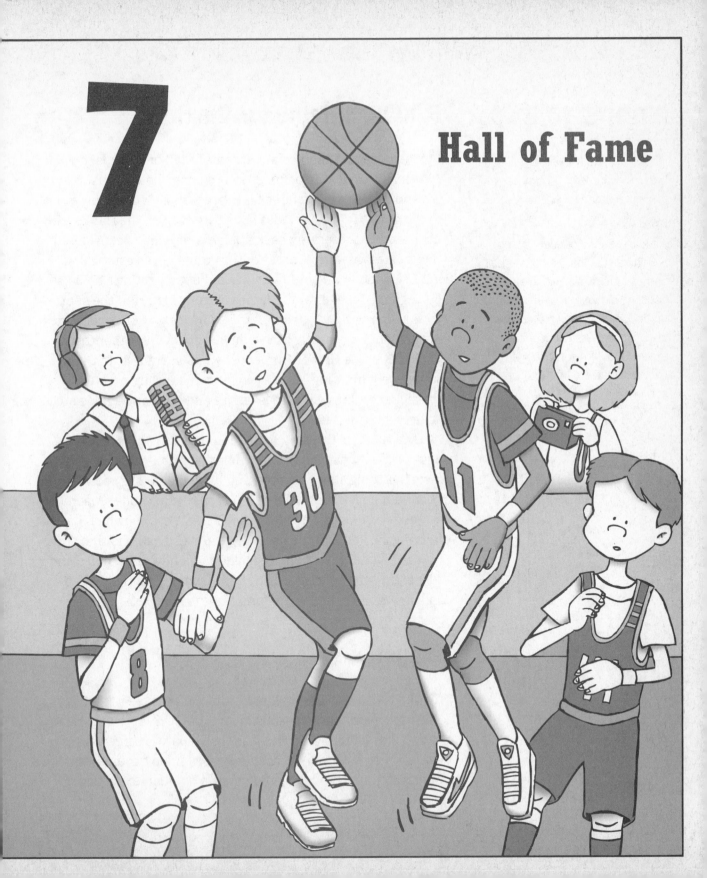

7

Hall of Fame

WORDS TO KNOW

Induction

Induction means a person is put into the Hall of Fame or "enshrined" or made a member of an institution.

Analyst

An analyst sits alongside the play-by-play announcer at a basketball game and explains why players or coaches did what they did. Often, former coaches and players make the best analysts because they experienced the same things during their own careers that the coaches and players are doing.

Finding a Home for the Hall

The Naismith Memorial Basketball Hall of Fame is in Springfield, Massachusetts, and enshrines not just players and coaches but referees and other major contributors to the game. It also includes six entire teams. The Hall is dedicated to preserving basketball history and is considered the greatest historical asset of the game. It was established in 1959, though an actual facility did not open until 1968 at Springfield College, where James Naismith started the sport with peach baskets as an effort to build teamwork and keep his students physically active during cold winter months.

In 2002, the Hall of Fame opened its current 80,000-square-foot building. As they approach, fans are greeted by the sight of a huge silver basketball and an orange globe atop sky-reaching spires.

The Hall has three floors. The Honors Ring overlooks the entire Hall. It has photos and a display of Hall-of-Famers's artifacts including shoes, jerseys, and basketballs. The second floor has the Players Gallery, the Hooperactive Zone, Coaches Gallery, Broadcast section, and College section, which has most of the items in the hall. There are also exhibits that show how the game was invented, including handwritten notes and speeches from Naismith. The Hall's Center Court features a full basketball court where fans can shoot baskets.

Induction

The Naismith Hall of Fame is unique because it includes international professionals and both U.S. and international amateurs. The Hall has four separate screening committees for American candidates, female candidates, international candidates, and veteran candidates. Veteran candidates have been retired at least 35 years before being nominated.

To be eligible for the Hall of Fame, players must be retired for at least five years. Referees must either be retired for five years or have at least 25 years as a referee at the high school, college, amateur, or professional level. No specific criteria exist for contributor inductees, but the person must have made a "significant contribution" to the game of basketball, and has included several famous broadcasters and sports writers. Contributors who have been inducted into the hall of fame include broadcasters like Dick Vitale, who has been an analyst with ESPN for more than 30 years.

The Naismith Hall also decides and presents several awards to collegiate players each year. The Bob Cousy Award has been presented since 2004 to the top point guard selected from Divisions I, II, and III. The Frances Pomeroy Naismith Award is presented to the female player less than 68 inches in height and male player less than 72 inches in height determined to have been that year's top student athlete. The men's award is voted on by the National Association of Basketball Coaches; the women's award is voted on by the Women's Basketball Coaches Association.

WORDS TO KNOW

Honors Committee
An Honors Committee of 12 permanent members and a rotating 12-member committee made up of specialists vote on candidates. Anyone who receives 18 votes, or 75 percent, from the Honors Committee is approved for enshrinement in the Hall of Fame. The committee can decide not to consider a potential nominee who has damaged the integrity of basketball.

HALL OF FAME PLAYERS

Kareem Abdul-Jabbar, 1995
Nathaniel Archibald, 1991
Paul J. Arizin, 1977
Charles Barkley, 2006
Thomas B. Barlow, 1980
Richard F. Barry, 1987
Elgin Baylor, 1976
John Beckman, 1972
Walter Bellamy, 1993
Sergei Belov, 1992
David Bing, 1990
Larry Bird, 1998
Carol Blazejowski, 1994
Bernard Borgmann, 1961
William W. Bradley, 1982
Joseph R. Brennan, 1974
Alfred N. Cervi, 1984
Wilton N. Chamberlain, 1978
Charles T. Cooper, 1976
Kresimir Cosic, 1996
Robert J. Cousy, 1970
David W. Cowens, 1991
Joan Crawford, 1997
William J. Cunningham, 1986
Denise Curry, 1997
Drazen Dalipagic, 2004
Robert E. Davies, 1969
Forrest S. DeBernardi, 1961
David A. DeBusschere, 1982
Henry G. Dehnert, 1968
Anne Donovan, 1995
Clyde Drexler, 2004
Joe Dumars, 2006
Paul Endacott, 1971
Alex English, 1997
Julius W. Erving, 1993
Harold E. Foster, 1964

Walter Frazier, 1987
Max Friedman, 1971
Joseph F. Fulks, 1977
Lauren Gale, 1976
Harry J. Gallatin, 1991
William "Pop" Gates, 1989
George Gervin, 1996
Thomas J. Gola, 1975
Gail Goodrich, 1996
Harold E. Greer, 1981
Robert F. Gruenig, 1963
Clifford O. Hagan, 1977
Victor A. Hanson, 1960
Lusia Harris-Stewart, 1992
John Havlicek, 1983
Cornelius L. Hawkins, 1992
Elvin E. Hayes, 1990
Marques Haynes, 1998
Thomas W. Heinsohn, 1986
Nat Holman, 1964
Robert J. Houbregs, 1987
Bailey Howell, 1997
Charles D. Hyatt, 1959
Daniel P. Issel, 1993
Harry "Buddy" Jeannette, 1994
Earvin "Magic" Johnson, 2002
William C. Johnson, 1976
Donald Neil Johnston, 1990
K. C. Jones, 1989
Samuel (Sam) Jones, 1983
Edward W. Krause, 1975
Robert A. Kurland, 1961
Robert J. Lanier, 1992
Joe Lapchick, 1966
Nancy Lieberman, 1996
Clyde E. Lovellette, 1988
Jerry R. Lucas, 1979

Angelo Luisetti, 1959
Hortencia Marcari, 2005
Robert McAdoo, 2000
Branch McCracken, 1960
Jack McCracken, 1962
Robert McDermott, 1988
Kevin McHale, 1999
Edward C. Macauley, 1960
Moses Malone, 2001
Peter P. Maravich, 1987
Slater N. Martin, 1981
Richard S. McGuire, 1993
Dino Meneghin, 2003
Ann E. Meyers, 1993
George L. Mikan, 1959
Vern Mikkelsen, 1995
Cheryl Miller, 1995
Vernon Earl Monroe, 1990
Calvin J. Murphy, 1993
Charles C. Murphy, 1960
Harlan O. Page, 1962
Robert Parish, 2003
Drazen Petrovic, 2002
Robert L. Pettit, 1970
Andy Phillip, 1961
James C. Pollard, 1977
Frank V. Ramsey, 1981
Willis Reed Jr, 1981
Arnold (Arnie) Risen, 1998
Oscar P. Robertson, 1979
John S. Roosma, 1961
John D. Russell, 1964
William F. Russell, 1974
Adolph Schayes, 1972
Ernest J. Schmidt, 1973
John J. Schommer, 1959
Barney Sedran, 1962

HALL OF FAME

Uljana Semjonova, 1993
Bill W. Sharman, 1975
Christian Steinmetz, 1961
Maurice Stokes, 2004
Isiah Thomas, 2000
David Thompson, 1996
John A. Thompson, 1962
Nate Thurmond, 1984

John (Jack) K. Twyman, 1982
Westley S. Unseld, 1988
Robert P. Vandivier, 1974
Edward A. Wachter, 1961
William T. Walton, 1993
Robert Wanzer, 1987
Jerry A. West, 1979
Nera D. White, 1992

Leonard (Lenny) Wilkens, 1989
Dominique Wilkins, 2006
Lynette Woodard, 2004
John R.Wooden, 1960
James Worthy, 2003
George Yardley, 1996

HALL OF FAME COACHES

Forrest Clare Allen, 1959
W. Harold Anderson, 1984
Arnold "Red" Auerbach, 1968
Geno Auriemma, 2006
Leon Barmore, 2003
Justin M. (Sam) Barry, 1978
Ernest A. Blood, 1960
Jim Boeheim, 2005
Larry Brown, 2002
Jim Calhoun, 2005
Howard G. Cann, 1967
Henry Clifford Carlson, 1959
Louis P. Carnesecca, 1992
Bernard L. Carnevale, 1969
Pete Carril, 1997
Everett N. Case, 1981
Van Chancellor, 2007
John Chaney, 2001
Jody Conradt, 1998
Denzil (Denny) E. Crum, 1994
Charles J. Daly, 1994
Everett S. Dean, 1966
Antonio Diaz-Miguel, 1997
Edgar A. Diddle, 1971
Bruce Drake, 1972
Pedro Ferrandiz, 2007

Sandro Gamba, 2006
Clarence E. Gaines, 1981
James H. (Jack) Gardner, 1983
Amory T. Gill, 1967
Aleksandr Gomelsky, 1995
Sue Gunter, 2005
Alexander (Alex) Hannum, 1998
Marv K. Harshman, 1984
Don Haskins, 1997
Edgar S. Hickey, 1978
Howard A. Hobson, 1965
William "Red" Holzman, 1986
Henry P. Iba, 1968
Phil Jackson, 2007
Alvin F. Julian, 1967
Frank W. Keaney, 1960
George E. Keogan, 1961
Robert M. Knight, 1991
Mike Krzyzewski, 2001
John Kundla, 1995
Ward L. Lambert, 1960
Harry Litwack, 1975
Kenneth D. Loeffler, 1964
Arthur C. Lonborg, 1972
Aleksandar Nikolic, 1998
Mirko Novosel, 2007

Arad A. McCutchan, 1980
Alfred J. McGuire, 1992
Frank J. McGuire, 1976
Walter E. Meanwell, 1959
Raymond J. Meyer, 1978
Ralph H. Miller, 1988
Billie Moore, 1999
Lute Olson, 2002
John (Jack) T. Ramsay, 1992
Cesare Rubini, 1994
Adolph F. Rupp, 1968
Leonard D. Sachs, 1961
Bill W. Sharman, 2004
Everett F. Shelton, 1979
Dean E. Smith, 1982
Pat Head Summitt, 2000
Fred R. Taylor, 1986
John Thompson, 1999
L. Margaret Wade, 1984
Stanley H. Watts, 1986
Leonard (Lenny) Wilkens, 1998
Roy Williams, 2007
John R. Wooden, 1972
Phil Woolpert, 1992
Morgan Wootten, 2000
Kay Yow, 2002

Lost in a Crowd

When you're a famous sports figure everybody knows what you do. Look at this crowd of people and see if you can pick out the famous players. They have 1 stripe on their shorts, a headband, and 2 long socks.

Most places around the world use the same word for basketball as we do, but some languages have their own word. In Italian it's *basket*. In Polish it's *koszykówka*. In Portuguese it's *basquete*, and in Spanish it's *baloncesto*.

HALL OF FAME

HALL OF FAME TEAMS

Buffalo Germans, 1961

The First Team, 1959

The Harlem Globetrotters, 2002

Original Celtics, 1959

New York Rens, 1963

Texas Western, 2007

The teams in the Hall of Fame include James Naismith's first team of 18 players who were studying at Springfield when James came up with the game of basketball. The team was inducted in 1959 at the inaugural induction and opening of the Hall of Fame. The Buffalo Germans were formed in 1895 at the Buffalo Eastside YMCA. In 1904, they won the National AAU Tournament, which served as an exhibition sport at the St. Louis Olympics.

An all-black team, the New York Renaissance, known also as the Rens, is also in the Hall. It was formed in 1923 by Robert Douglas. Though the team played home games at the Harlem Renaissance Casino and Ballroom, it became famous for barnstorming the nation, playing teams nationally. The team had a record of 112-8, winning 88 games in a row at one point. It was the first black team to win a national tournament, beating the National Basketball League's Oshkosh All-Stars. The Rens had a career record of 2,588-539 and disbanded in 1949.

Another great barnstorming team in the Hall of Fame is the Original Celtics (no relation to the Boston Celtics), which was a pro touring team in the 1920s. The team was an offshoot of the New York Celtics, with several players from that team and added players mostly from New York City's West Side. The team played in several fledgling leagues before deciding to tour nationwide, playing about 175 games a year. The team won 90 percent of its games, and its 1922–1923 record of 193-11-1 is still among the most awe-inspiring in basketball history.

FUN FACTS

From 1908 to 1911, the Germans won 111 games, which was an incredible total of victories, especially considering how new the sport was.

BASKETBALL HALL OF FAME "Great Sportcasters"

WORDS TO KNOW

Barnstorming
This means to travel around the country playing in small and big towns, wherever a game can be set up.

Double Duty

**This Hall of Fame is very unique . . .
or maybe not. There are two of them!
Can you spot the 7 differences?**

The team was forced to join the American Basketball League in 1926 because teams would not otherwise play the Celtics. The Celtics dominated the league so much in the first two seasons that the league disbanded the team and farmed out its players to other teams.

The Harlem Globetrotters, an entertainment act with basketball skill and verve, is another Hall of Fame team. It was formed in 1926 and has played more than 20,000 games in 118 countries as of 2008. The team's beginnings are disputed, but it is a favorite of fans worldwide, with amazing dribblers, crazy shots that always seem to go in, and a playfulness that delights spectators around the world. They also have a lot of talent. Early on, they beat the George Mikan-led Minneapolis Lakers in 1948 and 1949. Players like Marques Haynes, Meadowlark Lemon, Geese Ausbie, and Curly Neal won't soon be forgotten by anyone who caught these basketball ambassadors live.

The 1966 Texas Western team (now the University of Texas at El Paso) made history when coach Don Haskins became the first to start five black players in college basketball. Texas Western beat Adolph Rupp's powerhouse University of Kentucky in the national championship game, 72-65. The 2006 movie *Glory Road* is based on the 1966 Texas Western season.

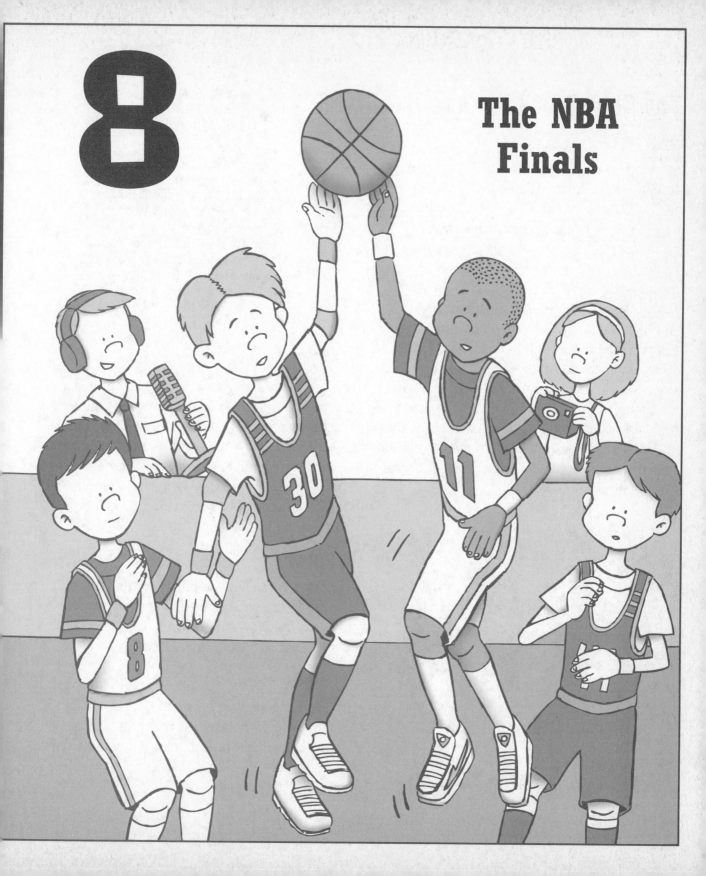

8

The NBA Finals

The Champions by Year

People remember players, but players remember league championships—in this case, the NBA Finals. You have heard someone ask, "But how many rings did that player have?" Fair or not, championships are the stick by which most of the great players are measured. Here's a brief rundown of the NBA Finals through the years. To get to the Finals, teams go through a series of playoff games. Eight teams in the Western Conference and eight teams in the Eastern Conference battle each other to get to the Finals. Teams play best of seven series; the first team in a series to win four games advances to the next round, and the loser is out of the playoffs. Eventually, there are only two teams left—one from each conference. These two teams play each other for the NBA championship.

1947

The Basketball Association of America's first league championship involved two of America's most famous cities, Chicago and Philadelphia. The Philadelphia Warriors of the Eastern Conference were led by future Hall of Famer Joe Fulks. They downed the Western Conference's Chicago Stags in five games, and Philadelphia claimed the league's first title.

1948

In a blow to Philadelphia's dominance, the Baltimore Bullets needed only six games to down the Warriors to win Baltimore's first league championship in a 4-2 series.

1949

Minneapolis Lakers center George Mikan became one of the league's first outstanding big men. George Mikan, 6 feet 10 inches, led his team past the Washington Capitols in a series that went six games, 4-2.

1950

In the 1950 finals, Minneapolis became the first repeat winner, downing the Syracuse Nationals, again in a six-game series, 4-2.

1951

The Rochester Royals and New York Knicks turned the basketball nation's eyes on the state of New York as Rochester won in a series that went the full seven games, 4-3.

1952

Two years after their repeat championship, the Minneapolis Lakers came back and made it count, beating the Knicks—who lost in the finals for the second year in a row—in another exciting seven-game series.

1953

The Minneapolis Lakers and Knicks had a repeat of the previous year's finals, and while the champion was the same—the Lakers—the series only went five games; the Knicks won just once.

1954

For the fifth time in the league's eight-year history, the Minneapolis Lakers claimed the league championships, surviving the Syracuse Nationals, 4 games to 3.

1955

After going to the league finals twice and losing, Syracuse finally got it together and claimed its first championship by defeating the Fort Wayne Pistons in seven games.

1956

Fort Wayne made it back to the finals, but the Pistons once again came up a little short. The Philadelphia Warriors claimed their first title since winning the inaugural championship, easily beating the Pistons 4-1.

1957

This was the start of something special for Boston. The Celtics made their first time to the finals count, beating the St. Louis Hawks in a series that went the full seven games.

1958

In a feel-good story that would last only one year, the St. Louis Hawks returned to the finals and beat the Boston Celtics in six games.

1959

The Celtics were back on track and rolled to their second title in three years, recording the finals first 4-0 sweep by beating the five-time league champion Minnesota Lakers.

★ FUN FACTS ★

The Rochester Royals are still around today, although they're not known by that name. The franchise has moved all over the country, playing in Cincinnati and Kansas City before becoming the Sacramento Kings in 1985. Their 1951 title is still their only one.

Tag Team

In basketball, each player has to be top notch, but it's even more important to be a team player. Can you match each team with its correct city?

Houston	Raptors
Seattle	Heat
Atlanta	Pistons
Los Angeles	Knicks
Toronto	Sonics
New York	Bulls
Boston	Hawks
Detroit	Lakers
Orlando	Magic
Chicago	Celtics
Miami	Rockets

What's the difference between a dog and a basketball player?

One drools and the other dribbles!

THE NBA FINALS

1960

The Boston Celtics took on the St. Louis Hawks once again, and they needed all seven games to win their third title in four years. The league's first true dynasty had kicked into high gear.

1961

Though the proud St. Louis Hawks made it back to the finals, they were but a speed bump for Boston, beating the Celtics only once in a series that went five games as the Celtics made it three in a row.

1962

In a preview of what fans would see decades down the road, the Boston Celtics took on the Los Angeles Lakers, and Boston came away with its fourth title in a row and its fifth in six years. But it wasn't easy—the series went the full seven games.

1963

Boston and more Boston. The Celtics needed six games to dispatch the Los Angeles Lakers and win their sixth overall title and fifth in a row.

1964

This time another California team, the San Francisco Warriors, battled the Celtics, but the result was a 4-1 series win for the Boston Celtics.

1965

The Los Angeles Lakers squared off against their familiar nemesis, the Boston Celtics. The Celtics needed just five games to claim their seventh title in a row.

1966

The Los Angeles Lakers put up a fight against the Boston Celtics and pushed the series to seven games. But in the end, the Celtics snagged their eighth title in a row.

1967

The Philadelphia 76ers eliminated the Celtics in the division finals, four games to one. They needed six games to beat the San Francisco Warriors in the finals, 4-2.

1968

The Celtics faced the familiar Los Angeles Lakers and Los Angeles fell in six games to the Celtics.

1969

The Boston Celtics got more than they imagined from LA's finals Most Valuable Player Jerry West—the first year the MVP was chosen—but the Lakers were not good enough to overcome the Celtics, as Boston won the league championship 4-3.

1970

After losing in the finals three times, the New York Knicks finally claimed their first league championship. Willis Reed won the Most Valuable Player award as he led the Knicks in a seven-game victory over Los Angeles.

WORDS TO KNOW

MVP

MVP stands for "Most Valuable Player." An MVP is named for the NBA Finals, the all-star game, and an overall NBA season. Depending on the rules for each particular award, the MVP is decided by the votes of members of the media or league officials, players, and coaches.

1971

A 7 foot 3 inch Kareem Abdul-Jabbar put the Milwaukee Bucks into their first NBA Finals. He was named the MVP of the series in a 4-0 sweep of the Baltimore Bullets.

1972

Wilt Chamberlain powered his Los Angeles Lakers to a 4-1 finals win over the New York Knicks.

1973

Led once again by finals MVP Willis Reed, the New York Knicks were too much for the L.A. Lakers and emerged victorious in five games.

1974

With a balanced cast of fundamentally deft players, the Boston Celtics and their tenacious defense, led by MVP John Havlicek, downed the Milwaukee Bucks in an exhaustive seven-game series.

1975

The Golden State Warriors brought Northern California and the Bay Area its first NBA Championship, as MVP Rick Barry led the Warriors to a sweep of the Washington Bullets.

1976

For the second time in three years, the Boston Celtics, on the cusp of rebuilding as a franchise, squeezed out another NBA Championship. Jo Jo White claimed MVP honors during the Celtics 4-2 rolling of the Phoenix Suns.

1977

Claiming their first—and so far, only—NBA Championship, the Portland Trail Blazers made the Pacific Northwest proud. The Blazers got the best out of Bill Walton and beat the Philadelphia 76ers in six games to claim the crown.

1978

The Washington Bullets, led by MVP center Wes Unseld, finally claimed an NBA Championship by halting the upstart Seattle SuperSonics in a series that went the entire seven games.

1979

For the second time in three years, fans in the Pacific Northwest had reason to smile, as the Seattle SuperSonics claimed their first NBA Championship. Led by MVP Dennis Johnson, the Sonics defeated the Washington Bullets 4-1.

1980

Magic Johnson, the MVP, keyed his Los Angeles Lakers to a 4-2 Championship over the Philadelphia 76ers.

1981

The Boston Celtics reclaimed their spot atop the heap with an NBA Championship. Cedric Maxwell won the MVP award by leading Boston past the Houston Rockets in a six-game final.

1982

Magic Johnson and the Los Angeles Lakers won their second title in three years by upending the Philadelphia 76ers, once again in six games.

1983

Making it to the NBA finals for the fourth time in seven years, the Philadelphia 76ers won their first NBA title since 1967, sweeping the Los Angeles Lakers 4-0. Moses Malone earned MVP honors.

1984

Larry Bird was named MVP as he led the Boston Celtics to an exciting seven-game win over the Los Angeles Lakers. It was only a preview of series matchups to come.

1985

Kareem Abdul-Jabbar was the cog that moved the Los Angeles Lakers machine to an NBA Championship, some 14 years after winning his first MVP award—no one else has ever had such a gap between MVP honors. The Lakers downed the rival Boston Celtics in six games.

1986

The Celtics made their third trip to the finals in three years. Behind Bird's second MVP performance, they downed the Houston Rockets in six games.

1987

This was the last of the great Celtics-Lakers matchups for 21 years. Magic Johnson won his third MVP award as the Los Angeles Lakers beat the Celtics 4-2.

1988

Los Angeles Lakers power forward James Worthy stepped up for an MVP, boosting Los Angeles past the Detroit Pistons in seven games.

1989

Though the Lakers made it back to the finals for the eighth time in 10 seasons, the Detroit Pistons were ready for them. Hot-shooting guard Joe Dumars earned MVP honors and sparked the Pistons to a sweep of the aging Lakers.

1990

The Detroit Pistons hit their third NBA finals in three years. Isiah Thomas earned MVP honors and boosted the Pistons over the Portland Trail Blazers in five games.

1991

Hello, Mr. Jordan. The Chicago Bulls officially became a force in the NBA, ending Detroit's dominance of the Eastern Conference. Michael claimed MVP honors by leading his team past the Los Angeles Lakers in five games, in a series that saw the Lakers make their last finals appearance until 2000.

TIP-IN

Michael is the third of five siblings. He has two older brothers and two younger sisters. His brother James retired in 2006 from the U.S. Army as the Command Sergeant Major of the 35th Signal Brigade of the XVIII Airborne Corps.

1992

The Bulls and Michael, again the MVP, dumped the Portland Trail Blazers in six games for Chicago's second title in a row.

FUN FACTS

Hakeem never even played basketball until he was 17 years old, yet he emerged as one of the most dominating centers in NBA history. Though he was—and remains—listed as 7 feet tall on all rosters and stat books, he admits he is barely taller than 6 feet 10 inches.

1993

The Bulls returned for their three-peat championship. Michael earned the MVP award for the third time in the Bulls's defeat of the Phoenix Suns.

1994

No Bulls? Not with Michael playing minor league baseball. The scrappy New York Knicks made the finals, but the Houston Rockets won the tough seven-game series 4-3. The Rockets's Hakeem Olajuwon claimed MVP honors.

1995

The world was introduced to the Orlando Magic's Shaquille O'Neal. But the veteran Houston Rockets swept the Magic in four games and took home the title. Hakeem was MVP.

1996

Michael rejoined Chicago late in the 1994–1995 season and led them back to the playoffs the next season. The Bulls beat the Seattle SuperSonics in six games, with Michael winning his fourth MVP award.

1997

Repeat alert: The Bulls, led by the one and only Michael, won a six-game series to down the Utah Jazz. His Airness earned another MVP.

1998

In a mirror image of the previous year's campaign, Michael was MVP as the Bulls beat the Utah Jazz for Chicago's second three-peat in eight years. It was Michael's sixth NBA Championship and sixth MVP award.

1999

Young Tim Duncan gave San Antonio the strong, big man to complement David Robinson. That was all the San Antonio Spurs needed to beat the New York Knicks in six games, with Tim earning MVP honors.

★ FUN FACTS ★

Michael's jump shot from the top of the key in the last game of the 1998 finals is a moment frozen in time for many fans. Michael retired after the win over Utah. Although he returned three years later with the Washington Wizards, he spent the height of his career with the Bulls.

TIP-IN

Not only did he represent his country in the Olympics, David served the United States in the Navy for two years after graduating from the Naval Academy and achieved the rank of Lieutenant, Junior Grade. He also scored the highest grade of any Naval Academy student in his gymnastics physical education class.

2000

The Lakers went from Magic and Kareem to Kobe and Shaquille, with Shaq claiming the MVP award in a six-game championship over the Indiana Pacers.

2001

The Philadelphia 76ers and Allen Iverson could not slow Shaq and his Lakers, who won in just five games. Shaq claimed MVP honors in the Lakers's second title in as many years.

2002

Good things come in threes, and for the third time since Michael won a pair of three-peats, Shaq led the Lakers past their third finals opponent. The Lakers won in a clean sweep over the New Jersey Nets. Shaq once again earned the MVP award.

2003

The Lakers's domination of the West came to an end as the San Antonio Spurs rose to the challenge. The Spurs cut down the New Jersey Nets in six games in New Jersey's second consecutive trip to the finals. Tim Duncan won his second MVP honor.

2004

In an Eastern team reminiscent of John Havlicek's balanced Celtics, the Detroit Pistons brought a balanced offense, keyed by MVP Chauncey Billups, to take down the Lakers in a quick five-game final.

2005

San Antonio got another MVP performance from Tim and survived a seven-game series with the defending champion Detroit Pistons.

2006

The Miami Heat signed Shaq for one reason: to win an NBA Championship. Dwayne Wade, the MVP, was the guard who ran the show and did most of the scoring as the Heat knocked off Dallas in six games.

2007

The San Antonio Spurs beat LeBron James and the Cleveland Cavaliers in a 4-0 sweep for San Antonio's third NBA crown in five years. Tony Parker nabbed MVP honors.

2008

The Celtics made a big push in the off season, signing perennial all-star Kevin Garnett away from Minnesota and getting hot-shooting Ray Allen to team with Paul Pierce. Boston was just too much for the Lakers, winning in six games as Paul earned MVP honors.

2009

The Los Angeles Lakers beat the Orlando Magic in five games. Kobe Bryant snagged the MVP award, but solid support from teammates Pau Gasol and Trevor Ariza sealed the championship. Lakers coach Phil Jackson earned his tenth championship ring, an all-time NBA record.

Flagging the Fakes

These teams all have their own flags. But it looks like somebody has slipped a fake one in with the real ones. Can you spot them?

ACTIVITY
You can design your own flag. Get a rectangular piece of paper and some crayons. You could use a family crest, a pet portrait, or anything you like. Just have fun!

Around the World

Europe has its own basketball teams. Can you pick them out from this jumble of letters?

Armani
Barcelona
Cibona
Joventut
Olimpija
Partizan
Prokom
Real
Unicaja

```
OLIMPIJACI
PLPARTIZAN
BARPRKUNCJ
REALKJOVDT
ARMANIOLIM
KOJOVENTUT
CIBONAANOB
BARCELONAB
PROKOMCAJO
OLIUNICAJA
```

Eight of the Top Teams in NBA History

Fans like to talk about their favorite teams—especially if their teams are highly successful teams. The ultimate sign of a successful team is one that has won multiple championships, either in consecutive years or during a particular era. Those teams are known as "dynasties" because they dominate the league during a certain period.

1964–1965 Boston Celtics

Bill Russell, Sam Jones, John Havlicek, Tom Sanders, and Tom Heinsohn led the Celtics to a 62-18 record. Boston broke its own league record for most victories in a season and went on to win the Celtics's seventh consecutive NBA championship. And it was only the beginning. Boston went up against the Philadelphia 76ers in an unforgettable Eastern Conference Finals, winning Game 7 110-109. John's deflection at the end of the game produced the famous broadcasting call, "Havlicek stole the ball!" The Celtics went on to defeat the Western Conference champion Los Angeles Lakers 4-1 in the 1965 NBA Finals.

1966–1967 Philadelphia 76ers

The Sixers went 68-13, led by Wilt Chamberlain, Hal Greer, Chet Walker, and Billy Cunningham. Philadelphia started the season 46-4 and went on to set a record for most victories in a season (though that mark was eclipsed by the 1971–1972 Los Angeles Lakers). This memorable season also put an end to Boston's run of eight consecutive championships. The 76ers slammed the Celtics 4-1 in the Eastern conference finals before going on to down the San Francisco Warriors 4-2 in the 1967 NBA finals.

1969–1970 New York Knicks

With a record of 60-22, this team had a lot of talent for the ages. Willis Reed, Walt Frazier, Dick Barnett, Dave DeBusschere, Bill Bradley, and Cazzie Russell starred for one of the best passing teams in NBA history. This group of Knicks claimed New York's first NBA championship by defeating Los Angeles 4-3 in the memorable 1970 NBA finals. Team leader Willis, who had missed Game 6 because of a leg injury, literally limped onto the Madison Square Garden floor before Game 7 and scored New York's first two baskets to inspire the Knicks to a 113-99 victory.

1971–1972 Los Angeles Lakers

Finishing the regular season with a record of 69-13, Gail Goodrich, Jerry West, Chamberlain, Jim McMillian, and Happy Hairston combined to bring the Lakers their first championship since relocating from Minnesota to Los Angeles. The Lakers broke Philadelphia's 1966–1967 record for wins in a season (which would later be broken by Chicago in 1995–1996). The Lakers also won 33 consecutive games during the regular season for a record that still stands. The Lakers also won an NBA record 16 consecutive road games and have the best road-win percentage in NBA history (.816; 31-7). The Lakers easily outplayed New York in the finals, winning 4-1.

1982–1983 Philadelphia 76ers

A memorable group of uniquely talented players inspired Philadelphia to a 65-17 season, as Moses Malone joined the 76ers as a free agent and teamed up with Julius Erving, Andrew Toney, Maurice Cheeks, and Bobby Jones to bring Philadelphia its first NBA championship in 16 seasons. Moses famously proclaimed that the 76ers would sweep through each round of the playoffs in four games, the minimum number of wins needed to advance in a best-of-seven series. He wasn't far off.

WORDS TO KNOW

Consecutive
Consecutive simply means in a row or without interruption. So if you won 10 straight games, you won 10 consecutive games.

Best-of-seven series
A best-of-seven series means the first team to win four games is declared winner of the series. While that can happen in as few as four games, the series can't go longer than seven games. Even if the teams are tied at 3 wins apiece after 6 games, the team who wins the next game will advance.

Philadelphia needed a fifth game to advance to the finals over the Eastern conference runners up, the Milwaukee Bucks. The Sixers cruised to victory against the Lakers in four games in the first round of the playoffs and dispatched the Knicks in four games in the finals. They posted the best winning percentage in NBA playoff history at .923 (12-1).

1985–1986 Boston Celtics

Stung by a 4-2 loss to the Lakers in the 1985 finals, Larry Bird led the Celtics to a 67-15 record with a team that featured Robert Parish, Kevin McHale, Dennis Johnson, Danny Ainge, and a rejuvenated Bill Walton. The team earned the best record in franchise history and a 4-2 defeat of Houston in the 1986 finals. The Celtics had a 40-1 record at home, the best home-winning percentage (.976) in NBA history.

1986–1987 Los Angeles Lakers

During this 65-17 season, the Lakers reascended the NBA throne thanks to the high-flying fast-break style of Magic Johnson, Kareem Abdul-Jabbar, James Worthy, Byron Scott, A.C. Green, and Michael Cooper. Magic averaged a career-best 23.9 points per game and led the league in assists with a 12.2 average. The Lakers defeated Boston 4-2 in the 1987 finals after winning 11 of their first 12 games in the playoffs.

1988–1989 Detroit Pistons

These 63-19 bad boys went out swinging—win or lose. Isiah Thomas, Bill Laimbeer, Joe Dumars, Mark Aguirre, Vinnie Johnson, and Dennis Rodman combined to form the heart of one of the strongest defensive teams in the modern era. Even though they did not have a commanding center, the Pistons featured a potent three-guard rotation and a deep bench that rebounded and defended relentlessly. Detroit went 15-2 in the 1989 playoffs, including a 4-0 sweep of the Lakers in the 1989 finals.

WORDS TO KNOW

Winning percentage
You can figure a team's winning percentage by dividing the number of games won by the number of games played. So if your team played four games and won three, you divide 3 by 4 and get a winning percentage of .75.

WORDS TO KNOW

Triangle offense
A sideline triangle is formed by the center in the low post, the forward standing on a wing, and a guard in one corner. The other guard is at the top of the key and the remaining forward in the high post, creating a two-man game. The spacing allows for passing, though the defense's reaction ultimately dictates what the offense does.

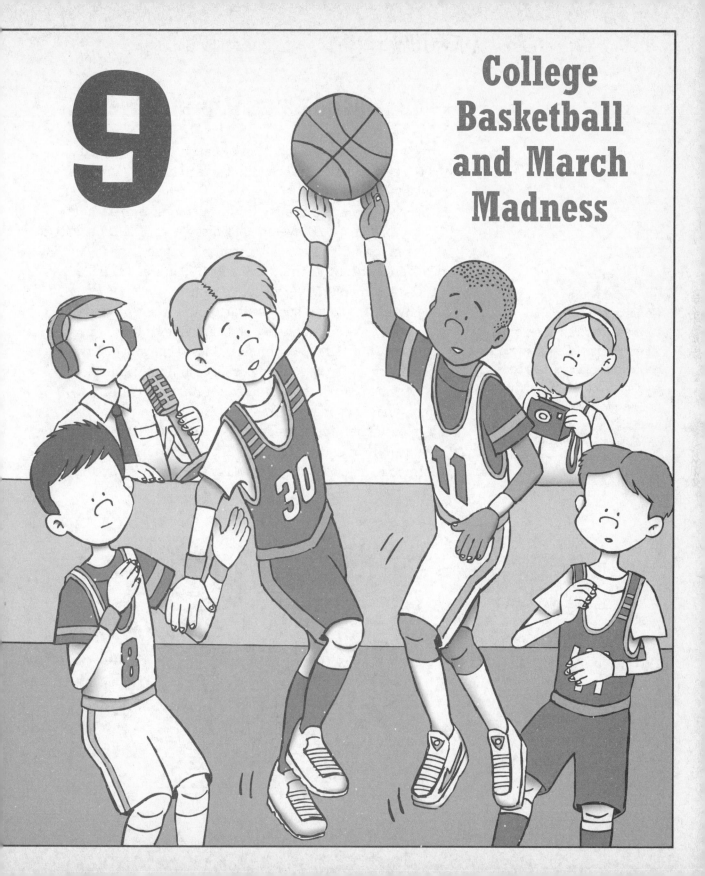

9

College
Basketball
and March
Madness

The College Game Migrates West

The first intercollegiate basketball game was played on February 9, 1895. The Minnesota School of Agriculture defeated Hamline College 9-3. Less than a year later, the first college game was played with the current five-men-on-the-court format. The University of Chicago beat the University of Iowa in Iowa City 15-12. In Naismith's native Canada, McGill University beat Queen's University 10-6 in December 1902 in the first Canadian intercollegiate game.

By 1901, colleges such as Dartmouth, the University of Chicago, Columbia, Minnesota, Utah, Yale, and the Naval Academy started having men's games. That was just the beginning; by 1906, so many colleges and universities were playing basketball that conferences started to form.

Injuries occurred so frequently in the infancy of college basketball that President Theodore Roosevelt actually stepped in and suggested in 1910 that a governing body be formed to rule over the sport. This eventually evolved into the NCAA.

WORDS TO KNOW

Conference
A college conference is a collection of teams, usually from the same geographic areas. These conferences often grow so large that they are broken into divisions. For example, the Big 12 has northern and southern divisions and the Southeastern Conference (SEC) has eastern and western divisions.

Women's basketball began in 1892 when Smith College hired physical education teacher Senda Berensen, who visited Dr. Naismith to learn more about the game of basketball. In 1893, Berensen had her Smith College freshmen and sophomores play each other in what is believed to be the first college women's game. She adapted the rules to better suit the women's game and published those in 1899. The first women's intercollegiate game was played in 1896. Stanford beat the University of California 2-1, and each team kept nine players at a time on the court.

March Madness

College basketball kept growing and growing through the years. While college football has the bowl season after the regular season, college basketball came up with a tournament all its own.

The NIT and NCAA Tournaments

In 1938, the Metropolitan Basketball Writers Association came up with the first college basketball tournament. They called it the National Invitation Tournament. Originally it had six teams, but over time it grew to include 40 teams. The NCAA tournament was created in 1939. It started with eight teams and grew to 65. The NIT and NCAA tourneys of the 1930s really changed the dynamic of college basketball because the tournaments allowed teams from all over the country to face one another and determine the best team in the nation. The NIT and NCAA tournaments were actually viewed as equal events until the late 1970s.

In 1950, the City College of New York won both the NCAA Tournament and the National Invitational Tournament. Doing well in these tournaments helped teams recruit the

TIP-IN

Though the NIT started out as a big deal, it is now the consolation prize for teams that do not make the 65-team NCAA tournament. Still, the NIT is a way for teams that didn't make the NCAA tourney to end the year on a high note, and it's always a treat for fans to see teams with good records battle each other.

★ FUN FACTS ★

If you're good at math, you've probably realized that four regions of 16 teams adds up to 64 teams. So where does the 65th team fit in? In 2001, the tournament decided to add one more team. In what's called the play-in game, this team battles the weakest 16 seed for the right to play in the tournament.

best players. Some of the schools that do well in the early days of the tournaments are still powerhouses today, including UCLA, North Carolina, Duke, and Indiana. Kansas, whose program was started by Naismith himself, was another early powerhouse; it won its most recent NCAA title in 2008.

March Madness

Each spring, millions of people enjoy an incredible month of college basketball: the modern NCAA tournament. In the late 1970s, the NCAA tournament established itself as the premier event and the NIT took a back seat. Sixty-five teams, ranked according to their strength, are invited to compete in the NCAA tournament. The top four teams receive a 1 seed, the next four strongest teams receive a 2 seed, and the ranking continues all the way down to the 16 seeds. Then the teams are divided into four regions of 16 teams.

The tournament is set up so that the strongest seeds play the weakest seeds. The 1 seeds play the 16 seeds, the 2 seeds play the 15 seeds, and so on. This is why it's a big boost for a team to be a high seed; they face the teams with the weakest records who will probably be the easiest to beat. The team that loses is out of the tournament and the winner advances to the next round. Because of this format the tournament moves quickly. Forty-eight games of basketball are played in the first four days of the tournament; that's a total of 32 hours of basketball—if none of the games go into overtime!

If the tournament were set up perfectly, the higher seeded team would always win and advance to the next round. In reality, this never happens. There are always upsets, and that's part of what makes watching the tournament so much fun. Every year people fill out brackets and try to predict when teams will win and lose. They compare their guesses with their friends and compete to see who can get the most right.

★ FUN FACTS ★

The seeding system started in 1979. In all the years since, a 16 seed has never knocked off a 1 seed. In 2008, all four 1 seeds (North Carolina, UCLA, Kansas, and Memphis) made it to the Final Four—the first time that had ever happened.

Confusing Recruits

This college team is recruiting new players by sending out an e-mail, but it looks like some letters got mixed up on the way. Can you figure out what the message says? Here's a hint: The letters T, E, A, and M have been replaced with other letters.

Hollo Biskocbill Lovors,

Wo will bo visicing your cicy cho lisc Cuosdiy of chis ponch. Wo iro looking for sopo now playors. Copo ouc and soo if you iro good onough co join cho coip!

Koop shoocing!

—Cho Coich

RATING RECRUITS

Blue chip is the term used to describe a top player coming out of high school who is being recruited.

The Top NCAA Men's Teams of All Time

Certain colleges and universities are known for their legacies of strong basketball programs. UCLA, for example, has won a mindboggling 11 NCAA championships. But a few individual teams made such an impact on the game that they can be considered the best of all time.

1976 Indiana Hoosiers

The University of Indiana Hoosiers went 32-0 in 1976, the only Division I team that has ever gone undefeated. Led by coach Bobby Knight, the Hoosiers beat the defending champion UCLA Bruins in the Final Four and won the national championship in a game against their Big Ten rivals, the Michigan Wolverines. Indiana won its regular season games by an average of more than 17 points a game and had two All-Americans in Scott May and Quinn Buckner.

1992 Duke Blue Devils

The 1992 Duke men's basketball team had superstars in Christian Laettner, Bobby Hurley, and Grant Hill, but they played as a team the whole season. They were the defending national champions, and Mike Krzyzewski coached them to a 34-2 record in the regular season.

The top seeded Blue Devils breezed through the NCAA tournament—until they ran into Rick Pitino's Kentucky Wildcats in the Elite Eight. The two teams battled their way into overtime and Duke trailed 103-102 with only 2.1 seconds remaining. Christian caught a long pass from Grant, dribbled once, turned to the basket, and hit a 17-foot jumper to put the Blue Devils ahead just as time ran out.

★ **FUN FACTS** ★

The movie *Hoosiers* is loosely based on the true story of a small-town high school team in Indiana that beat a big-city school for the state championship.

Duke eked out a three-point win over Indiana in the Final Four and then ran away with an anticlimactic championship game against the University of Michigan's much hyped freshmen starters, the Fab Five.

1996 Kentucky Wildcats

After losing to Duke in the 1992 Elite Eight, Rick Pitino led his Wildcats to a Final Four appearance in 1993. But his best team was the 1996 Wildcats, who went 34-2 and featured future first-round NBA picks Antoine Walker, Tony Delk, Walter McCarty, Derek Anderson, and Ron Mercer. The Wildcats were at their best in the NCAA tournament, winning their six tourney games by an average of more than 20 points each.

1982 North Carolina Tar Heels

The 1982 University of North Carolina team had players like Michael Jordan, Sam Perkins, and James Worthy. None of their opponents could figure out how to stop their powerful offense. The Tar Heels went 34-2 in the regular season and advanced to the national championship game against Georgetown. With 17 seconds remaining in the game, Michael launched a 17-foot jumper to clinch a 63-62 victory for the Tar Heels.

1974 North Carolina State Wolfpack

The 1974 North Carolina State Wolfpack went 30-1. It was led by highflying David Thompson, who would go on to star for the Denver Nuggets, and 5 foot 6 inches point guard Monte Towe. The Wolfpack could win any way needed, beating Maryland 103-100 for the Atlantic Coast Conference title and then taking down UCLA 80-77 in the NCAA semifinals before finishing it off with a 76-64 NCAA championship win over Marquette.

FUN FACTS

In the 1982 title game, future NBA rivals Michael Jordan and Patrick Ewing faced off against each other. Three years earlier, Magic Johnson's Michigan State Spartans defeated Larry Bird's Indiana State Sycamores in the most-watched title game ever. The Bird-Magic rivalry continued in the NBA, where they met in the finals in 1984, 1985, and 1987.

1968 UCLA Bruins

John Wooden's 1968 UCLA team lost to the University of Houston in the middle of the season but came back to trounce the same team in the NCAA tournament—by 32 points. UCLA had Lew Alcindor, who averaged 26 points and 16 rebounds a game. The Bruins downed North Carolina 78-55 to win the NCAA tournament.

1972 UCLA Bruins

John's 1972 UCLA Bruins dominated the landscape like no other team, before or since. They earned a perfect 30-0 record and beat opponents by an average of more than 32 points per game during the regular season. The team featured future NBA Hall of Fame center Bill Walton, who would later claim he was "embarrassed" by his play as UCLA beat Florida State by five, 81-76, in the NCAA championship game that year.

> **TIP-IN**
>
> Kareem owns eight UCLA records, including most field goals (943), most points in a season (870), and most points in a single game (61).

The Greatest College Players

Some of the greatest college players went on to become NBA superstars. Others didn't find as much success in the NBA, but fans still remember their biggest collegiate moments.

Lew Alcindor (Kareem Abdul-Jabbar)

Lew Alcindor, later Kareem Abdul-Jabbar, won three consecutive championships at UCLA in 1967, 1968, and 1969. Freshmen were not allowed to play on varsity, but Lew was so dominating he led the freshmen team past the UCLA varsity, which was ranked No. 1 in the nation at the time. He was named NCAA tournament Most Valuable Player all three years he was eligible and was the first winner of the Naismith College Player of the Year award in 1969.

College Copies

There are a lot of college basketball players with very similar skills. Sometimes they're so close it's hard to tell them apart! Can you see the 10 differences here?

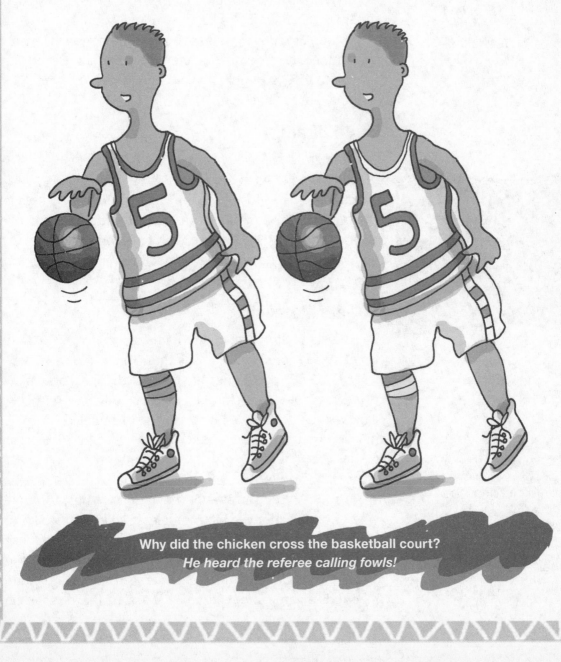

Why did the chicken cross the basketball court?
He heard the referee calling fowls!

Bill Russell

Bill Russell would go on to become one of the great players of all time, but coming out of high school he only got one letter recruiting him. It was from a local school, the University of San Francisco. Bill arrived as a diamond in the rough and immediately became a defensive standout. He led San Francisco to 55 straight wins, including the 1955 and 1956 national championships.

Bill Bradley

Though he originally committed to Duke, Bill Bradley opted instead to go to Princeton University for an Ivy League education. The 6 foot 5 inch Bill was a three-time All-American and scored 58 points in an NCAA tournament win over Wichita State in 1965. Bill went on to become a U.S. Senator and was a candidate for the Democratic Presidential nomination.

Pete Maravich

Louisiana State University had a scorer in Pete Maravich. No one had scored more points than Pete when he left college with 3,667 points, despite the fact that he'd only played three years because freshmen were not eligible. In 83 college games, Pete averaged 44.2 points a game and led the NCAA in scoring three times.

Jerry West

Jerry West put the eyes of the nation on West Virginia when he played for the Mountaineers, leading the team to the 1959 NCAA Finals as a junior and earning the tournament's MVP award—even though his team lost. He played 1958–1960, and in his final year averaged 29.3 points and 16.5 rebounds a game and recorded 134 assists for the season.

Elvin Hayes

Elvin Hayes was one of the first African American players for the University of Houston. Elvin led Houston to the NCAA Final Four in 1967, scoring 25 points and grabbing 24 rebounds in a semifinal loss to eventual champ UCLA. The following year, Houston and UCLA played each other in the first nationally televised college basketball game, in which Elvin scored 39 points, recorded 15 rebounds, and kept Lew Alcindor to just 15 points.

Jerry Lucas

Jerry Lucas turned down basketball powerhouse Kentucky to go to Ohio State University; he was from nearby Middletown and earned an academic scholarship to Ohio State. The Buckeyes went 78-6 in his three years of varsity play. Jerry directed Ohio State to three finals, including the national championship in 1960, and became the only player to ever score 30 points and have 30 rebounds in the same game.

Christian Laettner

Christian Laettner will always be known for his buzzer-beating shot from the top of the key to beat Kentucky in the 1992 NCAA East regional. Christian played in four consecutive Final Fours for Duke University and still has the record of having played in 23 NCAA tournament games. He owns the records in the NCAA tournament for most points scored (407) and most free throws made (142).

Team Effort

Here's a new team, but it doesn't have a name yet. Can you figure out which is the correct one? It must have:

- at least one S
- at least one I
- at least one B
- only one word with two syllables

Dribble Kings

Leapin' Lizards

Hoop Hogs

Basket Masters

Passing Princes

Jumping Giants

★ FUN FACTS ★

Michael called David his favorite player growing up. David was a Number 1 draft pick of both the ABA and NBA, but signed with the Denver Nuggets of the ABA.

WORDS TO KNOW

Win streak
A win streak is how many victories in a row a team has. A losing streak is the number of defeats in a row a team has suffered.

David Thompson

David Thompson led North Carolina State to a perfect 27-0 season in 1973 when the team was not eligible for the NCAA tournament. The next year, he came back and led the Wolfpack to the NCAA title, beating defending champ UCLA. David and teammate Monte Towe are largely credited with inventing the alley-oop, where the ball is passed to someone in mid-flight and dunked. Called an idol by no less than Michael Jordan, David's jersey number 44 is the only one retired by NC State.

Oscar Robertson

Oscar Robertson averaged 33.8 points per game at the University of Cincinnati, the third highest in college history. In three varsity seasons, Cincinnati was 79-9 and made the Final Four twice. Oscar set 19 school records and 14 NCAA records.

Bill Walton

Bill Walton was a big force for UCLA from 1971 to 1974, leading the team to back-to-back NCAA titles in 1972 and 1973. In the 1973 title game win over Memphis, Bill made 21 of 22 shots from the field and scored 44 of UCLA's 87 points, which is widely regarded as the best single-game title performance of all time. Bill was also a key figure during UCLA's record 88-game win streak.

Glossary of Terms

Air ball

A shot that does not hit the rim; misses everything.

Alley-oop

A pass is made to a forward who slam dunks the ball into the hoop. A spectacular and crowd-pleasing play.

Alternate possessions

In college and high school, this rule substitutes for a jump ball during the game only (not at the start of the game). So if two players have possession of the ball at the same time—both have hands on it—the referee will blow the whistle. The official scorer keeps track with an arrow at courtside that shows whose turn it is to have possession, and it rotates back and forth. So the team that is awarded possession the first time will not get it the second time, but will get it the third time, and so on.

Arc

The trajectory of a shot; the three-point line is also called the three-point arc.

Assist

A pass that sets up a successful basket. The player who made that pass is credited with an assist.

Backboard

The glass, metal, or synthetic board the hoop is bolted to. It can also be used to bank in shots, from the outside, layups, or free throws.

Backscreen

An offensive player moves away from the basket to set a screen for a teammate who either has the ball or is trying to get free for a pass.

Ball fake

Used to distract opponents, it can be a fake pass or shot.

Ball handler

The player who has the basketball; usually moving the ball up the court, it is the point guard.

Ball hog

Someone who does not pass the ball to teammates and takes most of the shots.

Bang the boards

A term used for trying hard to get rebounds; also called "crashing the boards."

Bank shot

A ball that goes off the backboard into the hoop. The backboard is thus used to "bank" the ball into the hoop by knowing right where to bounce it off the backboard so it goes into the hoop.

Baseball pass

A pass thrown with one hand.

Baseline

The line that runs the width of the court behind each basket that signifies out of bounds.

Basket interference

Touching the basketball while it is in any part of the "cylinder" or on the rim of the basket, reaching through the basket to touch the ball, or pulling down on the rim as an illegal defensive maneuver.

Behind-the-back pass

Bouncing the ball from one hand to the other behind one's back.

Block

A shot that is knocked away.

Bounce pass

Bouncing the ball on the floor, usually once, while making a pass to a teammate.

Box out

Putting your body between the defender and the basket to keep them from getting rebounds.

Brick

A shot that misses badly by clanking hard or awkwardly off the rim or backboard.

Buzzer-beater

A shot that goes in just before time expires.

Carrying

When a player dribbling the ball temporarily stops and then continues. In effect, it is traveling and is similar to a double dribble.

Catch and face

The term used to get a pass and square up to the basket to shoot, done in one motion to allow the defender no time to react.

Center

The tallest player on the team, counted on to score baskets from in close, to win jump balls, block opposing players' shots, and get a lot of rebounds.

Charge

When an offensive player runs into a defender whose feet are planted.

Charity stripe

A nickname for the free throw line.

Chest pass

A two-handed pass thrown from the chest.

Clear out

Offensive player or players moving out of an area so a teammate with the ball can try to move toward the basket.

Crossover dribble

Dribbling from one hand to the other; can be used to fake defenders about what direction the ball handler wants to go.

Cut

An offensive move often toward the basket or an open spot on the court to get away from a defender.

Cylinder

The area above the rim; once the ball enters that area it cannot be touched or it is goaltending.

Defensive rebound

If your opponent misses a shot and you get the ball it is a defensive rebound because it came at the end of the court you are defending.

Double-double

When a player has double figures (10 or more) in points and rebounds.

Double dribbling

When a player is dribbling the ball then stops, and then starts again. The other team gets possession of the ball.

Double team

When two defenders guard a single player to prevent him from getting the ball or scoring.

Dribbling

Bouncing the ball up and down—required to move with the basketball.

Driving

Dribbling the ball toward the basket.

Fadeaway jumper

Jumping backward at a slight angle while taking a shot. It is very hard to block.

Fast break

Moving the ball quickly up the court and not allowing defensive players to set up. Often results in outnumbering the defensive team momentarily if done fast, allowing a player an open or unguarded attempt to score.

Field goal

Any shot other than a free throw.

Field goal percentage

The number of shots (not including free throws) made divided by the number attempted. So if you took four shots and made two, you'd have a field goal percentage of 50.

Finger roll

Not as popular as it was in the 1980s, this involves scoring a "lay-in" or layup by letting the ball roll off the fingers.

GLOSSARY OF TERMS

Five-second violation

When inbounding the ball, the player trying to do it has to pass the ball inbounds within five seconds or the opposing team gets possession.

Flagrant foul

A foul made on purpose with too much physical contact or force, resulting either in automatic free throws or the player being thrown out of the game.

Flex offense

An offensive scheme designed in the 1970s that involves a lot of motion, screens, and cuts in the offense. Though it is considered too predictable to be used in the pros or even college, the plays are easy to remember and involve all players, so it is still used in kids' leagues as a way to teach basic skills.

Flop

A player exaggerates being contacted by an opposing player to try to get the referee to call a foul.

Foul

Illegal contact with an opponent: reaching in for a ball, jumping over a player's back for a rebound, running into a player trying to score if his feet are planted, or if the defender is moving when the collision occurs are some.

Foul line

The line 15 feet in front of the basket where free throws are attempted.

Foul out

Depending on the level of play, five or six fouls result in the player no longer being allowed to play in that particular game.

Four-corners

A type of offense where players form a square in the offensive end while the player dribbling the ball is in the middle. By using screens and cuts, the team is trying to get a good shot attempt or layup.

Free throw

Shots taken after a foul by the opposing team. The game is stopped and the player is allowed to shoot one, two, or as many as three uncontested free throws, which are always worth one point each.

Free throw percentage

The number of free throws made divided by free throws attempted. A good free throw shooter makes at least seven or eight out of 10, and some players in the NBA make at least 90 percent of their free throws.

Full-court press

Using defensive pressure to cover the team with the ball the whole length of the court, from the time they inbound it all the way to the offensive end of the court.

Garbage time

When the outcome of the game is already decided because a team leads by an undefeatable amount of points and not enough time is left for the losing team to catch up. This is when coaches "clear the bench" and put in mostly substitutes.

Give and go

An offensive play where the player with the ball passes to a teammate and then cuts or otherwise takes off toward the hoop and gets the ball right back.

Goaltending

When the ball is on a downward arc into the basket or on the rim and is interfered with by a defender and the offensive team is awarded points whether the ball goes in or not.

Hook shot

Most often done by centers, though occasionally done by other players, when the player is perpendicular to the basket and sweeps the ball toward the basket in a hook motion, making it hard to defend or block.

Inbounds pass

The team with the ball has one player stand out of bounds and that player tries to pass it to one of her four teammates on the court.

Jump ball

The ball is tossed in the air and the best jumpers or tallest players from each team jump and try to tip it to a teammate; used to start a game.

Jump shot

Used with a field goal; the player jumps, usually straight up, as part of the shooting motion so that a defender cannot block the shot. This replaced the set shot.

Key

The shaded rectangular area in front of each basket that goes out to the foul line, shooting line, and half-circle where players stand to shoot free throws. In international basketball, the lane is shaped more like a trapezoid.

Lane violation

During a free throw attempt, entering the lane too early, before the ball has hit the rim. The lane is the shaded area in front of the free throw line.

Layup

A two-point shot made from in close from either side of the basket, banked off the glass and into the basket. One of the most successful shots attempted if the player is open; however, it is also often blocked by taller players. Though often done off a fastbreak, it can also be done when a player becomes open near the basket.

Man-to-man defense

Each player guards another player on the opposing team, following that player everywhere on defense and trying to keep that player from receiving passes or taking shots.

Matchup zone

A combination of a zone defense and man-to-man defense. Defensive players match up with specific offensive players, while other defenders play zone and are responsible not for certain players but particular areas and guard only players who enter the zone they are responsible for.

Mikan drill

A popular drill at tryouts, preseason practices, and basketball camps. Standing under the basket, the player makes a layup with the right hand and catches the ball after it comes through the hoop and net with the left hand. Then the player makes a layup with the left hand and catches the ball with the right hand. Named after one of the NBA's first dominant big men, George Mikan.

Motion offense

Uses player movement to move the defense around and get offensive players open to make baskets. Often it is used to single out a weakness of the defensive team or to best use one of the strengths of the offensive team. Heavily used to create shooting lanes or lanes to drive to the basket. Particularly effective against taller or slower opponents.

Net

The white nylon or mesh that hangs from the hoop. A ball "swishes" through the net if it is shot so precisely that it does not touch the rim, creating the term "Nothing but net" for a really good shot.

One and one

These are given for nonshooting fouls. If the player makes the first shot, he gets a second shot. If he misses the first one the ball is live and in play.

Overtime

An extra period of time to play if the score is tied at the end of regulation play; also known as OT. Points scored in overtime count just as they would for any other time during the game.

Paint

The shaded area of the key in front of the free throw line.

Pass

Using any kind of throw or chest pass to get the ball to a teammate.

Penetration

When a player dribbles the ball into the paint toward the basket.

Perimeter

The area outside the lane. Players who shoot from behind 15 feet are often called perimeter shooters and players who rarely go into the paint are called perimeter players.

GLOSSARY OF TERMS

Period

A quarter in a four-quarter game. A half is divided into two quarters each at the professional level. Any game that goes into overtime is called an overtime period.

Personal foul

Illegal contact with an opponent, ranging from pushing or putting hands on players to running into them

Pick

Setting a screen for a teammate.

Pick and roll

A player sets a screen (also called a pick) for the ball handler, then the screen setter slips behind the defender to get a pass from the ball handler.

Pivot

Rotating your body around one planted foot kept in a stationary position. As long as that one foot stays planted, a player with the ball can pivot left or right, toward or away from the basket.

Point guard

The Number 1 spot on the floor, the player who dribbles the ball up the court and sets up the offense. Though there are now taller point guards, traditionally the point guard is smaller, has good knowledge of the game, and gets a lot of assists by finding the open teammate to set up baskets.

Points

These are used to keep score of the game. A free throw is worth 1 point, field goals (including layups and dunks) inside the three-point arc are good for 2 points, and baskets shot with both feet behind the three-point arc are awarded 3 points.

Post

The area on either side of the free throw line. The low post is closer to the basket and the high post is closer to the free throw line. Centers usually play in the low post.

Post up

Taking a position close to the basket, facing away from the basket, and getting between the defender and the teammate with the ball to create a passing lane to receive the ball.

Power forward

Referred to as the Number 4 spot. A power forward can rebound and play inside and has the size and strength to get a lot of offensive and defensive rebounds, but score a lot on offense.

Princeton offense

Princeton devised an offense to capitalize on its fast, smaller players. It uses constant motion, screens, backdoor passing, cuts, and a lot of hustle. Players are also required to know the fundamentals well and be "smart" or "thinkers" on the court. The backdoor

pass is often used for easy layups as defenses get disoriented and drawn out of position by the Princeton offense.

Putback

Getting a rebound off a missed shot by a teammate and immediately putting it back in for a 2-point field goal. Also called garbage points because they come from picking up others' mistakes (missed shots) or trash.

Quadruple double

Ten or more each from four of five of these categories: points, rebounds, assists, steals, and blocks.

Rebound

Getting the ball after it hits the rim on an unsuccessful shot on either the defensive or offensive end.

Reverse dribble

Changing direction while bouncing the ball.

Reverse pivot

The same as a pivot, only stepping backward with the nonstationary foot. This is used to take a shot or to draw in the defender so the offensive player can drive to the basket or draw a foul.

Screen

A move used to block a player to free up a ball handler or a player trying to get open to receive a pass or to attempt a shot. Also called a pick, it depends on timing and possession because a player who is moving while setting a screen can be called for a foul.

Shootaround

This is a casual practice where players shoot at one hoop in a halfcourt setting.

Shooting guard

The Number 2 spot on the floor; a guard who can shoot from the outside, especially three pointers.

Shot clock

Used to speed up the pace of a game and prevent teams with a lead from stalling or running out the clock. Forces teams to take a shot that at least hits the rim (or goes in) within a set amount of time, usually 24 seconds or 30 seconds, but occasionally 35 depending on the level of play. If a team fails to take a shot that at least hits the rim in the allotted shot clock time, the whistle is blown and possession is turned over to the opposing team.

Sidelines

The longer lines on each side of the court that indicate where out-of-bounds and in-bounds are.

Sixth man

The player who is not among the five players to start the game, but is the first player off the bench to substitute into the game for one of the starting five. This became such an important role that the NBA came up with an award for the best sixth man each season.

Slam dunk

A field goal worth 2 points, but is often exciting for fans as a player jumps up into the air and forces the ball through the hoop with his hand touching or grabbing the rim as the ball is forced in. This is also a hard shot to block. Abdul-Jabbar became so proficient at this that it was banned by the NBA for nine years from the late 1960s to mid 1970s and is a favorite of both fans and television stations that show highlights.

Small forward

Usually bigger than the guards but smaller than traditional forwards, a player who is a good shooter, quick, and can drive to the basket with the ball.

Spin dribble

Turning around to "shake off" a defender or prevent a steal while bouncing the ball; used to change direction.

Squaring up

When a shooter's shoulders face the basket in preparation for a shot attempt.

Starting lineup

The five players who are on the floor to start the game.

Steal

When a defensive player, without fouling, successfully takes possession of the ball from the offensive player. Can be done by taking the ball, batting or deflecting a pass to a teammate, or intercepting a pass.

Strong side

The side of the court where the ball is at that time. If the ball goes to the other side, that becomes the strong side.

Substitution

When a player from the bench is put in for a player on the court. This is done throughout the game, so substitutes are often themselves substituted out of the game.

Swing man

A player who can play the Number 2 shooting guard position to Number 3 small forward position.

Technical foul

A foul called for technical reasons or unsportsmanlike conduct, whether it is arguing with referees, getting in the face of an opponent, or instigating a brawl; called when the ball is not in play.

Ten-second line

When the halfcourt line is used to enforce the team with the ball to move it from their defensive end to the offensive end within eight seconds of getting possession for the NBA; 10 seconds for college.

Three-point field goal

Shot from behind the three-point arc, a field goal worth 3 points. In the

GLOSSARY OF TERMS

NCAA the arc is 20 feet 9 inches from the basket; in the NBA it is 23 feet 9 inches.

Three-point play
When the offensive player is fouled making a field goal and makes the 1-point free throw awarded for the defender's foul.

Three-second violation
Offensive players must move in and out of the shaded area in front of the free throw line; failing to move in and out of the key, standing in it for three seconds or more, results in a turnover.

Timeout
Usually by coaches to discuss strategy or to figure out a strategy if the opposing team has made several baskets in a row.

Tip-off
The jump ball at center court that starts a game. Often used in schedules or media reports as the "tip off" time for a game.

Top of the key
The area at the end of the free throw circle and the only place to shoot a three pointer facing the basket head on.

Transition
When a team quickly goes from defense to offense; a good opportunity to get uncontested layups or open outside shots after getting possession of the ball.

Trap
A defensive technique when at least two players swarm the player with the ball to force a turnover.

Traveling
Most commonly called when a player takes too many steps with the ball while not dribbling.

Triangle offense
A sideline triangle is formed by the center in the low post, the forward standing on a wing, and a guard in one corner. The other guard is at the top of the key and the remaining forward in the high post, creating a two-man game. The spacing allows for passing, though the defense's reaction and attempts to defend it is what dictates what the offense does. Though it is seen as too complex for younger players, this "path of least resistance" offense, once mastered, can create gaudy scoring numbers if operated with the right players.

Triple-double
Getting 10 or more points each in scoring, rebounds, and assists.

Turnover
This can result from the offense having the ball stolen, from an intercepted pass or one thrown out of bounds, traveling, or getting called for an offensive foul. All of these result in the ball being turned over to the opposing team.

Walking
Another term used for traveling. If a coach sees an opposing player travel and the referee does not call it, the coach will call out, "He walked!"

Weak side
The side of the court without the ball.

Zone defense
Rather than have each player guard a player on the opposing team, players are responsible only for certain areas on the defensive end of the court. There are several variations on the zone and it is created to either counter an opposing team's strengths or to minimize a team's own weaknesses.

Resources

Movies

High School Hero, 1927
Campus Confessions, 1938
The Basketball Fix, 1951
Tall Story, 1960
Hoosiers, 1986
Blue Chips, 1994
Hoop Dreams, 1994
Annie O, 1995
Celtic Pride, 1996
Eddie, 1996
Soul in the Hole, 1996
Space Jam, 1996
The 6th Man, 1997
Air Bud, 1997
The Basket, 1999
Finding Forrester, 1999
Michael Jordan, An American Hero,
    1999
New Jersey Turnpikes, 1999
Passing Glory, 1999
Crossing the Line, 2002
Something to Cheer About, 2002
Coach Carter, 2005
Glory Road, 2006

Magazines

Basketball Digest

Includes articles and features on all leagues professional and college, has player profiles and statistics. Much like the "digest" magazines for other sports, it's everything basketball in every issue.

Bounce

Covers the sport and includes features such as ranking the top playground tournaments, consistent with its self-declared image as a grass-roots magazine that hopes to be something for players at every level, not just fans of pro and college teams.

Dime

Includes feature stories on players, reviews of shoes, and updates on players.

ESPN the Magazine

A magazine designed for everything related to sports; especially during the college and professional basketball seasons, it has a lot of information on college and NBA basketball.

Slam

A comprehensive basketball magazine that began publishing in 1994 that combines hip-hop culture with basketball and includes a letters-to-the-editor section called "Trash Talk."

Websites

HoopsVibe.com

Has NBA News and Rumors section updated throughout the day, blogs, reviews of basketball shoes, and other items.
www.hoopsvibe.com

InsideHoops.com

Has constantly updated news headlines, player movements, and other breaking news from professional and college basketball.
www.insidehoops.com

NBA.com

The official source of news, features, and statistics for the NBA. You can find anything related to the NBA on this site, from schedules for this year to standings and biographies of current and former players.
www.nba.com

APPENDIX C
Puzzle Answers

CHAPTER 1: PLAYING THE GAME
Name That Position • page 4

Shooting guard (usually best ball thrower from a distance)

Small forward (tend to be versatile)

Center (usually tallest and slowest)

Power forward (usually not as tall as the center)

Point guard (usually shortest and fastest)

Same But Different • page 16

Lists of Lists • page 24

Sports with the letter B in them: baseball, ballooning, handball, badminton, bungee jumping, basketball, T-ball, powerboating, racquetball, snowboarding

Sports equipment: shoulder pads, knee pads, helmet, goggles, flippers, skip rope, wrist guard, baseball bat, catcher's mitt, ski pole

Cities that have hosted the Olympics: Los Angeles, Innsbruck, Beijing, Atlanta, Nagano, Barcelona, Seoul, Sydney, Turin, Calgary

Sports where you don't kick a ball: hockey, golf, diving, tennis, lacrosse, squash, swimming, water polo, ultimate Frisbee, skiing

CHAPTER 2: HISTORY OF THE GAME
Lucky 13 • page 31

1. Opening an umbrella indoors
2. Putting shoes on the table
3. Letting a black cat cross your path
4. Walking under a ladder
5. Stepping on a crack

Do What Coach Says • page 35

⅔ will get on the team (8 out of 12)

Inflated Basketball • page 37

$20 = $500 $32 = $800
$27 = $675 $50 = $1250

CHAPTER 3: GREAT PLAYERS OF YESTERDAY
Court Count • page 43

Point Well Taken • **page 51**

Bounce Back • **page 57**

React	Remote
Reposition	Recline
Return	Remodel

CHAPTER 4: GREAT PLAYERS OF TODAY
Matching Sets • **page 63**

Opposites Attract • **page 71**

win/lose	professional/amateur
run/walk	player/worker
best/worst	tall/short
average/extraordinary	push/pull
major/minor	

Score! • **page 72**

OBASTALBLCSKRE

TKELSBCERALBOS

OCASSTABLLEEBKE

RALOKESCCASTBLE

KCLEOASBABSLRET

ALTLSBRSSEOAECK

KBSABCSLELEROAT

PUZZLE ANSWERS

CHAPTER 5: WOMEN'S BASKETBALL
Three's a Charm • page 76
15 times

Pick Up the Pieces • page 79

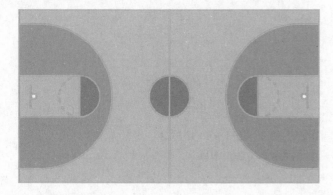

Amazing Athletes • page 83

```
    C H E R Y L M I L L E R
        I
        S U E B I R D
        A
N A N C Y L I E B E R M A N
S H E R Y L S W O O P E S
        L
        I
    R E B E C C A L O B O
T A M I K A C A T C H I N G S
```

Tally Ho! • page 84
20 + 40 + 10 + 3 = 73
25 + 25 + 15 + 6 = 71
34 + 10 + 8 + 10 + 10 = 72
11 + 11 + 11 + 11 + 25 = 69
1 + 1 + 60 + 3 + 13 = 78
22 + 22 + 22 + 10 = 76
9 + 9 + 9 + 27 + 26 = 80
16 + 10 + 10 + 10 + 10 + 23 = 79

CHAPTER 6: COACHES
Follow the Rules! • page 87

Everybody Chant • page 89

The game is on, it's getting late
The score's close, 87 to 88
It's up to you to decide their fate!
Make us proud of our state;
Let's tell the players we think they're great!

Crazy Coach • page 91

Run round robin regularly
Don't dribble downtown
Perfect players play politely
Tonight tall teams take turns
Grateful guards get goals

CHAPTER 7: HALL OF FAME
Lost in a Crowd • page 98

Double Duty • page 100

CHAPTER 8: THE NBA FINALS
Tag Team • page 104

Boston Celtics	Houston Rockets	Detroit Pistons
Chicago Bulls	Atlanta Hawks	Orlando Magic
Los Angeles Lakers	Toronto Raptors	New York Knicks
Miami Heat	Seattle Sonics	

Flagging the Fakes • page 111

PUZZLE ANSWERS

Around the World •
page 112

OLIMPIJA
   PARTIZAN

REAL
ARMANI
  JOVENTUT
CIBONA
BARCELONA
PROKOM
  UNICAJA

**CHAPTER 9: COLLEGE BASKETBALL AND
MARCH MADNESS**
Confusing Recruits • **page 119**
Hello Basketball Lovers,
We will be visiting your city the last Tuesday of this month.
We are looking for some new players. Come out and see if
you're good enough to join the team!

Keep Shooting!
—The Coach

College Copies •
page 123

Team Effort • **page 125**
Dribble Kings